PLAY AND POWER

The EFPP Book Series

Series Editor: *Dimitris Anastasopoulos*

OTHER TITLES IN THE SERIES

PLAY AND POWER

Editors

*Karen Vibeke Mortensen
and Liselotte Grünbaum*

KARNAC

First published in 2010 by
Karnac Books Ltd
118 Finchley Road
London NW3 5HT

British Library Cataloguing in Publication Data

A C.I.P. for this book is available from the British Library

ISBN-13: 978-1-85575-803-2

Typeset by Vikatan Publishing Solutions (P) Ltd., Chennai, India

Printed in Great Britain

www.karnacbooks.com

CONTENTS

FOREWORD

Dimitris Anastasopoulos

Combining two apparently contradictory concepts is a challenge. This, however, is why it is interesting, as it involves us examining the specifics of each case and of the relationships between them more closely. In a way, I "re-read" this book, as I had already heard most of the papers presented at the Copenhagen Congress. In the serenity my office now offered, I delightedly discovered new facets which, in the busy flow of Congress, did not receive the attention they deserved.

Generally speaking, the book is an exceptionally enriching, multi-faceted approach to the subject. As it explores issues of developmental and psychic trauma, reaching all the way into the archaic, pre-mentalization play of recurrently traumatized children belonging to the so-called third world, the role of playing and its pro-hibitive or permissive relationship with power, is clearly outlined. In this exploration, a reference to hate (*Mette Kjær Barfort*) is added as a crucial point of convergence between the exertion of force and the ability to play within the therapeutic process and relationship, complemented by references to the father and finally, to groups and social institutions. Inspired by the content of the book, I will attempt to reflect on the issues it raises, propose certain ideas initially on

vii

play then around power, and finally comment on the way they interweave and interact with each other.

We begin with play, the more "innocent" of the concepts. Throughout the years, and mostly thanks to Winnicott, play has been unanimously considered as a cornerstone of child development, as very clearly described in this book.

Play is a symbolic expression of fantasies and reality as they are perceived. In addition, play itself has the power to symbolically realize said fantasies. In order for play to exist, freedom of action and expression is required. This occurs in the transitional intermediate space between phantasy and reality. Play development is linked with the primary process where it becomes oneiric, in the zone between the conscious and the unconscious. Play is the ability to relate within a world where phantasy and reality are temporarily merged. There, play and dreams almost identify with each other and are often confused with the child's reality.

Play is tightly connected with images affected by phantasy. It is connected to the development of unconscious thought, through the primary processing of phantastic and real data. One cannot control play; one can only stop it. From the moment of intervention through the force of reality, the expression of the phantasy, as well as symbolic expression, is inhibited. Play is almost equated with independence of will and unconscious exchange. It is free, expressive of emotions and ideas, and communicative.

In the therapeutic intervention with play, language is introduced, intersecting the imaginary, restoring the barrier between conscious and unconscious, promoting symbolization beyond the primary one used.

At times, play can take on a dramatic magnitude, when it is linked with a history of abuse and psychic trauma (*Liselotte Grünbaum*). Then, the internal drama is acted out. Sometimes it is difficult for the child to play. When he subsequently acquires this ability through psychotherapy, he plays in order to reconstitute his inner world, to overcome the disaster he has experienced and to reconstitute his internal objects into relationships and roles that make sense and are not destructive.

Language play is yet another way of mastering fears and anxiety, thus calming aggressiveness. The use of jokes and humor that Sigmund Freud pointed out are such examples.

The infant's archaic play, beautifully described in *Chantal Lheureux-Davidse's* chapter, structures the inner world and its relationship with the outside world little by little, while simultaneously removing annihilation anxieties.

On a social level, play is considered childish and portentousness; "serious-looking". A sterile rejection of play under the cover of responsibility, allow games to take its place. Games refer to a consciously organized and directed playing, in which unconscious phantasies are sometimes expressed. It can function as a tool for the relief of social tension or for guidance, but it rarely results primarily in creativity. It is interesting that in order to rediscover the connection with unrestrained creative thinking and fantasy, in institutions we often resort to "brain storming" which is a sort of an invitation, to a certain extent, to engage in free association and play of the mind.

From the other side, power provokes the individual to realize his childhood phantasies of omnipotence and of sadistic enforcement on external objects. It is a double-edged knife, because naked power by itself becomes malevolent and can transform into perversion and be anti-task. It needs to be linked with something which will facilitate its sublimation and halt its tendency to discharge in the form of a violent destructive force; this is dependent on the wisdom with which it is used. It is so close to survival instinct, that in order for it to function creatively it has to be bound and directed towards libidinal goals, with a care for the object.

The seductive issues pertaining to power are domination, submission, control, and having another to submit to our instinctual desires, the other finding himself at the mercy of the powerful. The power of destruction gives a feeling of immediate exercise of effective power and omnipotence. This does not allow for the development of relationships based on mutuality that will include care for the object. Power can become an object of admiration, attraction and desire, but never of emotional sharing and exchange.

During development, power naturally lies on the parents' side. When the child senses that power is being transferred onto him by a weak or over-investing parent, the shift from vulnerability to omnipotence might terrify him. There are no mature psychic mechanisms to transform this power into mental strength or promote object relationships of mutual care. The deviation towards raw violence and self-destruction as well as the destruction of others becomes an option, such as in the case of the child warriors who were created during the recent wars in Africa.

I would say that during the course of normal adolescent development, the mastery of newly acquired power plays an important role. The adolescent becomes significantly stronger than the parent, something that touches upon phantasies of incest and patricide, while still feeling emotionally vulnerable, experiencing the tendency not to abandon his position of dependence on the parents. The challenges posed by adolescence are connected with the management of this power and its re-direction along developmentally useful paths. I think this occurs through the use of play in relationships, through activities, music which tames phantasies, the promotion of relationships among and between sexes, the channeling of impetus and aggression and experimentation with roles. In sexuality, play will introduce pleasure, sharing and creativity. The exertion of power can lead to domination, competition and destruction or perversion.

Reference to the father is usually a reference to the power he has and his role as protector of the evolvement of developmental play between the mother and child is often misjudged. The father possesses the necessary power (penis/phallus) to protect, support and strengthen the child's efforts to conquer the world. The absent father, crucially stated in *Jacob Segal's* chapter, creates a lack of power, a void in the formation of the child's mental development; a void in the development of his confidence. The father's power is also necessary in order to modulate the power emergence of the phantasy and fusional archaic mother, possessing a benevolent power and introducing a third pole in the play of family relationships. His role, his knowledge and the rules of the setting give the therapist the power within the analytic relationship.

Analysis demands the ability for play and playfulness. Analytic thought is developed in an environment of maximum, within limits, freedom of expression, permissiveness and promotion of the development of phantasies and their cooperative symbolic processing. Winnicott is so familiar to us in many ways liberating us from guilt. We applaud his views on the importance of participative play and on the therapeutic procedure between therapist and patient and forget to extend his opinions backwards, back to the process of creating a psychotherapist of the psychoanalyst. We often do not even touch upon the self-evident; that psychoanalytic thinking and the therapist's ability to mentally "play" during a session require a setting of freedom of thought and speech in order to develop. Thus, sometimes within psychoanalytic associations and institutions, a power struggle dominates over freedom, the development of free thought which poses questions and seeks answers, and over the development of the analyst's ability to play.

The idea of acting out as a negative of play, which is introduced in *Peter Ramsing's* chapter on groups, is also very interesting. In this case, action aims at discharge; pleasure is not attributed to creativity, but takes on the form of comfort and relief from the unpleasant. Both are temporary and the acting out tends to become repetitive and actualizing not promoting phantasy life or sublimation. Acting out that concerns destructive phantasies can become dangerous to the self and the other. The other is no longer the companion in a mutual play, but an object to be used. Perhaps the ultimate anti-play in psychotherapy concerns the negative therapeutic reaction, by which power exerted with envy destroys and eliminates any creativity.

In analytic therapy there is a need for a certain degree of power to be exercised in order to maintain basic control; it is acceptable and required in order to maintain the setting, yet should not impact on the process. In *Monica Lanyado's* chapter we witness a child relinquishing the power she had acquired, through a tremendous effort by the therapist, as a tactic to avoid separation. One can distinguish an idiomorphic power game between them, as noted by *Liselotte Grünbaum* in which the therapist responds to the use of power as a means to further the goals of the therapy.

Uncontrolled, unlimited power results in violence, abuse and distortion.

Uncontrolled, unlimited play results in the loss of being in touch with reality and an inability to use it in the construction of a phantasy world.

The use or abuse of that power will set the creative or destructive course of the therapy. The most important requirement is for the therapist to have the strength to endure and metabolize the powerful projections of the patient's destructive side. In a symbolic manner, by "playing" with him, he will guide him into using his mental strength creatively.

The social dimension of the relationship between play and power is introduced in *Gerhard Wilke's* chapter. Individuals who posses power can exercise this by applying their diagnostic systems and methods of choice, and force others to follow them. This is often a raw demonstration of the exertion of power that institutionally interferes with the application of free play-communication in psychoanalysis.

At the other end of the social spectrum we find that ideologies founded on power leave no room for freedom of expression of thoughts, desires, feelings, and subsequently play, since they aim for a controlled and directed human mind, resulting in the exertion of violence.

While play predicates mutuality, the exertion of too much power can strip off this character and transform it into a tool for defeat, subjection, control, and the use of the object for the narcissistic satisfaction of the subject's phantasies. In this case, play takes on a distorting form and negates itself, giving its place to the proto-symbolic, impulsive exertion of authority. When dominance becomes the goal, play is destroyed and excessive rivalry develops.

I hope I have managed to convey some of the rich and fertile dialogue stemming from the study of this book by *Liselotte Grünbaum* and *Karen Vibeke Mortensen* and I am overjoyed to have been given a chance to comment on it.

SOME BRIEF ORGANISATIONAL PERSPECTIVES

Anton Obholzer

It is rare for an essentially clinical book to include elements from an organisational perspective. This is probably on account of the fact that most clinical work takes place either in organisational settings, which are taken for granted, or in private consulting rooms where the organisational component is relatively minimal. For a "true picture" of the clinical case to emerge, it is helpful for there to be an overall perspective available in order to see the material in context. It is usual in clinical descriptions for there to be some mention of the family, sibling and peer relationships and possibly also some cultural perspectives. Institutional elements are however routinely ignored or at least neglected.

The image that I find most helpful as a metaphor for the overall picture is that of Russian Dolls in which a series of dolls, all of the same design, fit into each other to make up a whole, consisting of a number of dolls of various sizes. The clinical analogy is then of the child's inner world: the child in relation to the mother, in relation to the father and in relation to the parents. We also have the family situation and local group situation, after which comes cultural and school settings, followed by the community and society at large. Of course, somewhere in this is the institutional setting if the child is in therapy. It is in a way the equivalent of children giving their postal address ending with the world, the universe, infinity etc.

So why should we focus on the organisational setting? My view is that the organisational setting can influence the climate, to a substantial degree, in which the clinical work, as described in the various papers and clinical foreword of this book, takes place. Nobody would quibble with the idea that parents who have unresolved personal developmental issues, have difficulty helping their children resolve such self-same issues in their child's personal growth and development. Thus a parent, with say, unresolved midlife sexual or moral issues, might have difficulty in helping their child negotiate their adolescent sexual development.

The same principle applies to institutions. An institution that functions in a way that is not conducive to the development and creativity of its staff is not in a good position to create a climate in which clinical staff can create a facilitating climate for patient development and growth. At worst, the clinical staff in such a problematic institution have to act in some way as a "protective barrier" or "clinical membrane" to protect themselves and their patients from "noxious institutional pressures". So for example an institution that is run on authoritarian "target orientated" lines, is likely to contaminate the staff state of mind and therapeutic freedom and cast a negative shadow over the therapeutic process.

On the other hand, an institution that makes allowance for personal staff and therapeutic flexibility is likely to provide a better setting for growth, creativity and patient outcome measures. The latter example in no way excludes the institution, the staff and the patients being in touch with the social and financial reality of the institution and its social setting.

As referred to in the clinical foreword, power and authority lie along a spectrum from abuse to facilitation. Just as in the inner world of the patient and his or her manifestations of this in the outer world, so it is in institutions. Power and authority in whatever setting need to be assessed in terms of where and how they manifest themselves in relation to the above-mentioned perspective. The Klein/Bion concept of the Paranoid/Schizoid—Depressive Position spectrum provides a helpful tool in assessing the state of mind of the system and is particularly of use when looking at institutional functioning. The above concept has to be coupled with the Miller/Rice concept of the Primary Task. In this case the concept of the primary task is related to the task of the overall organisation as such. What is the purpose of the organisation and how does it need to structure itself to perform its task? The Jaques/Menzies conundrum follows on from the above. What is the pain and/or anxiety that arises from the work that the institution has to embark on and what unconscious defensive manoeuvres have the staff fallen into to protect themselves from, or to evade, the painful issues arising from the work?

Looking at the functioning of an institution and in the particular case we are concerned with here, namely the functioning of the institution in such a way that it facilitates the formation of a setting that is creative and constructive for both staff and patients, we need to consider the following: What are the underlying unconscious anxieties aroused by the nature of the work, i.e. raised by the "raw material" entering the institutional system? Thus in the cases described in this book, we are talking about the taking in of madness, of social malfunctioning and of violence, and mostly of disillusionment of the idea of growth and development as a normal happening to be expected.

These "attacks" on staff mental capacity and assumptions, cause staff to fall into defensive personal and institutional processes that act counter to the pursuit of the primary task of the institution. This latter task could generally be described as "to foster growth and development in all concerned". For this state of mind to prevail in the institution, there needs to be open acknowledgement of the "risk" to the staff when engaged in the work they are doing, as well as open communication and staff support systems to counter these anti-task phenomena. As mentioned above, the application of the paranoid-schizoid-depressive position parameters are helpful at this point.

An institution operating at the depressive position end of the spectrum has exactly the same qualities as an individual who essentially functions at the depressive end of the spectrum, more or less most of the time. This way of describing this state of mind implies that one might be in a certain state of mind most of the time but that it is normal sometimes to slide into the more primitive paranoid-schizoid position, to recover oneself to a degree, moving back into the more mature area of the depressive position.

So how would an essentially depressive position organisation function? It would, as mentioned above, be aware of its primary task; the risks associated with it, and have in place mechanisms to reduce the most problematic pressures arising from the work. It would have a realistic picture of what could and could not be achieved, given the task and the resources at hand to deal with them. It would forego an omnipotent, self-idealising or narcissistic self-image, while at the same time maintaining a positive attitude towards the work in the context of a longer-term, strategic horizon. The underlying question here is where would we as an institution like to be in five, ten or fifteen years time, and what do we need to put in place to enhance the chances of achieving these hoped-for goals? The above mentioned goals as linked to the previous mentioned metaphor of the Russian Dolls, is really not that different from what a couple would strive for in thinking about the development of their children. By contrast, a paranoid-schizoid approach would instead imply a veering between omnipotence and impotence, hope and hopelessness, and a management that fell into short-term, opportunistic adventures in conflict with the longer term, strategic aspirations.

Here a distinction also needs to be made between Authoritarian and Authoritative styles of management. An authoritarian style by and large, is short of consultation and long on leading by the imposition of power. It is thus suppressant of debate. An authoritative style gives clear leadership along the primary task and strategic development parameters as outlined above, and then implements decisions on that basis. In a paranoid-schizoid institutional climate, there is a much higher chance of the emergence of an authoritarian leadership style which in turn then affects the overall institutional staff and patient climate as mentioned previously. Staff are thus more likely to re-enact authoritarian and target driven elements in their contact with each other and with their patients.

It must however be recognised that one of the endemic problems in therapeutic institutions is that they are managed as if they were "therapeutic communities" for the benefit of the staff, as opposed to business organisations, in pursuit of the primary task. The hallmark of "therapeutic community" type management is often one of endless discussion with little decision making, implementation of decisions, or acting on deadlines. Just as in a family with endless discussion and no action, so in an institution, such behaviour should be recognised for what it is, namely anti-task and anti-development.

There are thus parallels between the intra-psychic requirements of the individual to have the best opportunities for growth and development, and for the institutions in which they are treated to have an equivalent institutional climate that acts as both a conscious and unconscious role-model and container for the work to proceed. The two processes need to go hand in hand for the best results to be achieved.

ABOUT THE AUTHORS

Dimitris Anastasopoulos (Greece), Dr., M.D., Ph.D., is a psychiatrist and child psychiatrist working in Athens. He trained in adolescent psychiatry and psychotherapy at the Tavistock Clinic, London and is a training and supervising psychoanalytic psychotherapist for adults as well as for children and adolescents. Until recently he was Vice Chairman and Child and Adolescent Section Coordinator of the European Federation of Psychoanalytic Psychotherapy (EFPP). He has been Chief Editor of the EFPP book series for the last two years. He is editor and author of many articles and books in Greek as well as in English.

Anton Obholzer (UK) is a child, adolescent and adult psychiatrist and Fellow of the Royal College of Psychiatrists in London. He is also a child, adolescent and adult psychoanalyst and member of the British Psychoanalytic Society. He was chairman of the Tavistock Clinic Adolescent Department and then Director of the Tavistock Centre, London from 1985 to 2003. He is an experienced organisational consultant and presently a senior member of faculty at the Global Leadership Centre, Insead Business School, Fontainbleau, France.

Mette Kjær Barfort (Denmark) has been a psychologist in private practice in Copenhagen since 1990. She previously worked in an adolescent psychiatric ward. She specialized in psychotherapy with personality disordered clients and trained as a supervisor with The Danish Society of Psychoanalytic Psychotherapy (DSPP). She trained and qualified as a psychotherapist with The Institute of Psychotherapy of Personality Disorders (IPPF), where she now works as a teacher and supervisor of psychologists and psychiatrists. She is a member of the boards of both DSPP and IPPF.

Chantal Lheureux-Davidse (France) is a lecturer in psychology at University Paris 7. She has had 13 years of experience in an institution for children and adolescents who were autistic, psychotic or handicapped with associated troubles. Autism was the topic of her doctoral thesis and together with addictions, creativity, the role of sensory sensibility in healing and construction of body image, has remained the main focus of her research since then. In 2003, her book, *L'autisme infantile ou le bruit de la rencontre,* was published by L'Harmattan. She has published in several scientific journals, such as Champ Psychosomatique, Cliniques Méditerranéennes, Psychologie Clinique, and Perspectives Psychiatriques. Being a board member of CIPPA (International Coordination of Psychotherapists with a Psychoanalytic orientation taking care of persons with Autism), she organises its working group which focuses on the emergence of language. Chantal Lheureux Davidse is in private practice as a psychoanalyst in Paris.

Liselotte Grünbaum (Denmark) is a registered M.Sc. in psychology, specialist and supervisor of psychotherapy and child psychology, in private practice in Copenhagen. She was a founding member and course organiser of the Danish Association of Psychoanalytic Child and Adolescent Psychotherapy and since 1997, has been a supervisor and teacher at the Danish training programme for Psychoanalytic Child and Adolescent Psychotherapists. She organised the child psychotherapy clinic at Aalborg University and is the clinic's supervisor. She is a member of the EFPP research group, former coordinator of this group and of the EFPP's Child and Adolescent Section. She has published a number of articles on psychoanalytic psychotherapy with severely deprived or traumatised children and adolescents, supervision of psychoanalytical psychotherapy and clinical psychology.

Jacinta Kennedy (Ireland), B.A., M.A., M. Psych. Sc., ECP, is a principal clinical psychologist and group analyst. She works in the Psychological Medicine Service at St. James's Hospital, Dublin and is a Founding Member and former Chair of the Irish Institute of Group Analysis. She is a teacher and supervisor on the Diploma in Group Analysis Course at the School of Psychotherapy, St. Vincent's Hospital, Dublin and a former lecturer in Psychology at Trinity College Dublin. Her teaching and research interests include work on depression in women, object relations theory, and she is currently conducting research in psycho-oncology.

Monica Lanyado (UK) trained at the Tavistock Clinic and was the founding course organiser of the Child and Adolescent Psychotherapy Training in Edinburgh. She is a training supervisor at the British Association of Psychotherapists and is joint Series Editor, with Ann Horne, of the Independent Psychoanalytic Approaches with Children and Adolescents Series. The first book in this Series, co-edited with Ann Horne, *A Question of Technique*, was published in 2006. Until recently Monica was also joint Series Editor, with Dimitris Anastasopolous, of the EFPP Book Series. As well as having written many papers, her publications include *The Presence of the Therapist: Treating Childhood Trauma* (2004) and, co-edited with Ann Horne, *The Handbook of Child and Adolescent Psychotherapy: Psychoanalytic Approaches* (1999).

Karen Vibeke Mortensen (Denmark), is a registered M.Sc. in Psychology, Dr. Pæd., and group analyst. She is an honorary Professor of clinical child psychology at Aalborg University and in private practice in Copenhagen. She is a specialist and supervisor of psychotherapy and child psychology and is supervisor and teacher on the Danish training programme for Psychoanalytic Child and Adolescent Psychotherapists. She has extensive teaching and supervision experience and has edited books and articles about various clinical and theoretical subjects, e.g., group analysis with children and adolescents, theories of psychopathology, assessment, research, and supervision of psychotherapy. Her doctoral thesis, *Form and Content in Children's Human Figure Drawings*, was edited by New York Univ. Press in 1991.

Peter Ramsing (Denmark), is a specialist in child and adolescent psychiatry and consultant at the Centre for Eating Disorders in

Aarhus. He received his diploma in 2004 for group analysis and since 1996 has been a teacher at the Group Analytic training programme in Aarhus. Since 2002 he has been a leader and teacher of a training programme in Child Psychotherapy in Aarhus. He has written chapters in Danish books about child and adolescent psychiatry and published an article in Matrix, a Nordic Journal for psychotherapy: *The Sound of Music, den Æoliske harpe og jagten på kreativitetens kilde* (The Sound of Music, the Aeolic harp and the hunt for the source of creativity).

Jacob Segal, Ph.D. (Israel), is a senior clinical psychologist, teaching at the Department of Psychology, Bar Ilan University and supervisor in Child Psychotherapy at the clinic of the Department of Psychology, Bar Ilan University. He is also a practicing adult and children psychoanalytic psychotherapist in full time private practice in Ramat-Gan, Israel. He is a trainee at the Max Eitingon Institute of Psychoanalysis, Jerusalem. His research includes loneliness and intimacy and the internal representations of object relations. He has written about supervision of psychoanalytic psychotherapy in a psychiatric hospital. He has a particular interest in the role of the father and the influence of the father's absence on the child's development and internal world.

Gerhard Wilke (UK), is a group analyst and member of the Institute of Group Analysis, London. He is also an Associate at Ashridge Business School in the UK and an independent organisational consultant. He studied Social Anthropology at King's College, Cambridge and became a psychotherapist after working in Adult Education in London. He believes that clinical knowledge is vital for an understanding of change in organisations and has spent the last ten years developing group analytic consultancy interventions. His work with clients has included individual and group coaching, leadership development, whole system development and the facilitation of difficult meetings and large groups. He is co-author of the best-selling book, *Living Leadership: a Practical Guide for Ordinary Heroes*, published by the Financial Times. He also studied and described the impact of the UK Health Reforms on doctors in *How to be a Good Enough General Practitioner*, published by Radcliffe Medical Press.

INTRODUCTION

Liselotte Grünbaum and Karen Vibeke Mortensen

At first sight the two words play and power may seem only to be connected by virtue of their first letter. On reflection however, they can both be recognized as central concepts in psychotherapy. But how are they related? An immediate reaction may be to see them as opposites. The first spontaneous associations may be mainly positive towards play and more ambivalent or perhaps even negative about power. Play may easily be connected with pictures of happiness, freedom and leisure, while power just as easily may be connected with hate, violence or abuse. Since the days of Winnicott, it is generally acknowledged that it is positive and even necessary to be able to play in psychotherapy. The good enough psychotherapist creates a playful space for the patient to play in, or, if the patient is unable to play, in which he may develop this capacity; therapists, therefore, must be able to play themselves. Play and psychotherapy may be directly connected as in play therapy. Associations with power in psychotherapy on the other hand, bring to mind thoughts about hate, envy, deadlock, power struggle, dominance, submission and destruction.

However, this picture may be turned upside down. What is presented as play may contain a powerful manic tendency that destroys closeness, seriousness and dedication. Consequently, the play becomes shallow and avoidant or even destructive. As such, it may be an expression of immaturity, a Peter Pan-refusal to grow up and an opposition to accept responsibility. The other way round, power may be a very benign concept, connected with energy, goal-direction and purpose. We talk about regaining our power if, for example, we have been ill. Without some investment of power, nothing much can be effected in the real world.

The relations between play and power are complex and manifold. Play needs power and play can give power back to the player. A pre-condition for this book is the premise that in order for helpful play and empowerment to develop in the therapeutic space, the benign power of the therapist is needed. You can play with your power in both a benign and a sadistic way. Both Winnicott and Melanie Klein describe as necessary for early, normal development, the ability of the mother to make space in the relationship, not only for love, but also for the child's powerful, aggressive phantasies about its objects (Winnicott, 1969; Klein, 1930, 1957). But it is certainly also true that violence and destruction have the power to annihilate play and even the ability to play. That is what has happened to so many of the children and adults we work with. Thus, we can think of psychotherapy as something that through the use of play, helps create strength and power in the patient again.

It is probably true that psychotherapists may be more inclined to talk about the necessity of the ability to play rather than the necessity of being powerful. Particularly in child psychotherapy, the choice of profession itself may be closely connected with the therapist's own pleasure in playing. But power is just as necessary as play in psychotherapy. For instance, the establishment and maintenance of a secure boundary around psychotherapeutic work may need quite a lot of power. The stability and perseverance that is needed by the psychotherapist in for instance, long-term psychotherapies with severely deprived persons, requires a lot of quiet but powerful endurance and personal authority.

Play and power can be explored in relation to psychotherapy: to what happens inside and around the therapeutic space in its narrow sense. But these can also be explored in the broader context of the community. In relation to society at large, are we as professionals able to maintain our power to play and be creative, or do we get stuck in fights and conflict, feelings of loss, and deprivation? Do we have and show, the power not only to stand up for what we believe in, but also to expand our field of activity? We need a lot of power to fight for our conviction that psychoanalytic psychotherapy offers vital help both to society and to many persons who cannot be helped in other ways.

The inspiration for this book was the sixth 3-section EFPP conference in Copenhagen in May 2007 with the main theme "Play and Power". At the conference and in the present book, this theme is presented both as inside and outside the therapeutic space. From the perspective of psychotherapy, play and power are elaborated in relation to group analysis, individual psychotherapy with adults and, child and adolescent psychotherapy. Perhaps it is characteristic that several of the psychotherapies described include extremely hateful or resigned children and adults who have been exposed to damaging or, in some other way, unhelpful environments. These case narratives demonstrate convincingly some of the devastating consequences that abuse of power in the real world may have. They also demonstrate how powerful the therapist needs to be in their conviction and endurance.

The contributions by Monica Lanyado and Peter Ramsing were presented as main lectures at the conference in Copenhagen, re-presenting child and adolescent psychotherapy and group analysis. The book starts with these two presentations. As main lectures, they were commented upon by discussants and we have chosen also to let their chapters in this book be followed by a short comment. Besides these contributions, the clinical part of the book contains one chapter on adult individual psychotherapy and four chapters on child psychotherapy. That this field of work presents the majority of the clinical contributions to the book is, probably, a consequence of the theme. Both play and power are conspicuously present in psychotherapy with children. The book is finally rounded off with two articles which explore power issues related to the broader societal and scientific base for psychotherapeutic work.

Through the case presentation of a young girl, Monica Lanyado explores the power of play to transform, how it can be the bridge to pleasure, joy and internal freedom, but also to unexplored depths of pain, deadness, and violence. She emphasizes how the gradual emergence of the ability to play is a very important milestone in the slow recovery of children who have been severely deprived or traumatized. The capacity to play is perhaps the best indicator of a child's level of emotional health and resilience in his internal world. But play is in itself, a very powerful vehicle for therapeutic change and can connect or reconnect the individual with his sense of true self. In the therapy, Monica Lanyado describes her attempts at being "playfully present" and giving "playful interpretations" as steps in the establishment of early contact. She also draws on knowledge from other fields such as neurophysiology and meditation.

In her comments on Monica Lanyado's chapter, Liselotte Grünbaum raises a number of questions, first about the role of play in the described psychotherapy. She emphasizes the significance of other important components in the psychotherapy, including the question of keeping in control while still respecting the survival strategies of the child and the introjection of a containing relationship as a precondition for the development of the ability to play. She raises among other points, the issue of interdisciplinary explanations; to which degree do they lead to fruitful qualitative developments or, to which degree may they result in just power play?

Peter Ramsing starts his chapter with some general reflections on the value of play. He then discusses positive and destructive forms of play in relation to experiences in analytic therapy groups. An example of destructive play from a therapy group is analyzed and its possible meanings explored. He adds other perspectives, such as a gender perspective and a mentalisation perspective, drawing on the concepts of psychic equivalence and the pretend mode, and shows how they can be useful in the understanding of group processes. Finally, he connects imaginative play to an archaic level of communication in the group, as described by Foulkes (1990), and to the Aeolian mode, as described by Cox and Theilgaard (1987).

In her discussion, Jacinta Kennedy raises the important question of whether it is always possible to distinguish between positive and negative play. She also stresses the necessity of not only manifesting maternal qualities, such as accommodation and containment, in group analysis, but also paternal qualities such as order, structure, and boundaries. There may be the need for thought-and-action, rather than thought and reverie. She points to the necessity of separating destructive fantasies from destructive acts and the need to try and limit negative play to fantasy. Finally, she discusses some important preconditions for the survival of a group in difficulties.

Mette Kjær Barfort raises the important question of how it is possible for the psychotherapist to maintain a playful, exploratory approach in their work when hate, envy and sadism dominate the therapeutic relationship. She describes some of the special characteristics of pathological hate, such as confusion between love and hate, the bond to past inner object relations, and its purpose in maintaining connection with the object. She refers to Rosenfeld's (1987) description of a special group of clients with destructive narcissism, obsessed with envy. The intensely hateful projections at times place the therapist in a position where they become overwhelmed by their own hateful feelings and lose sense of the analytic space. They may alternate between feeling powerless and being drowned in their own rage and hate, followed by feelings of guilt and shame. Consequently, symbolic thinking may break down. The problem for the therapist is not so much feelings of hatred towards the patient, which probably are impossible to avoid, but rather how they can be handled doing as little harm as possible.

Liselotte Grünbaum also emphasizes the power of play to overcome the destructive power of deprivation and trauma in early childhood. As illustrated in a therapy with a six year old severely traumatized girl, she focuses on the trauma-related inhibition of the ability for symbol-formation. She describes the fragmented, distorted and defective forms of play that arise in the therapeutic space and shows how periods of silent emptiness alternate with stereotyped repetitions and confusing fragments of symbolic play. Psychotherapy with such a child makes great demands on the therapist's ability to understand their countertransference feelings and accordingly, to wait patiently for symbolic thought to become possible in the therapeutic space.

Chantal Lheureux-Davidse describes a very difficult psychotherapy with an autistic, deeply handicapped boy without language. She shows how the autistic child's withdrawal of cathexis from his body in order to take refuge in his thoughts, results in a fragmentation of his sensorial world. This deprives him of his feeling of existence, communication becomes impossible and experiences of annihilation may arise. Through playing with the most archaic forms of communication such as vibrations, speed, rhythms and the intensity of sounds and movement, it becomes possible to get in touch and communicate her understanding to the boy to such a degree that he becomes able to feel his own existence and express himself in spoken language. It is a very moving demonstration of the very powerful effect of psychotherapy with some of the most severely handicapped children.

Jacob Segal writes about the unconscious return of the absent father and draws attention to the father as a primary object whose very existence and relationship with the mother and child, are critical for the child's emotional development. The absence of a father may produce a preoccupation with issues of power and vulnerability in the child. Through sessions from psychotherapies, he illustrates some characteristic forms of transference/countertransference relationships in psychotherapy with patients whose relation to their childhood father was a relation of absence. One type is the "detached father transference" in which the power of emotional detachment is very present. There is a distant relationship to the therapist, resistance to talking about their relationship, sometimes combined with devaluation and attacks. Conversely, the second type describes a powerful hunger for the therapist as a father-figure.

Gerhard Wilke extends the perspective to focus not only on the power dynamics between patient and psychotherapist, but also on the power play between modernists and traditionalists and between managers and clinicians in Public Health Organizations. He suggests that power and play are inter-subjective phenomena and that it is questionable to talk of power holders, such as managers and administrators, as perpetrators and of psychotherapists as victims in a powerless position. Psychotherapists are challenged to engage with a true, rather than a false self when engaging in power play with those whom they perceive as their competitors, controllers and managers. He argues that if we, as psychoanalytic psychotherapists, can put self-care before patient-care, we can resist submitting passively to the fate of being marginalized as a preferred treatment modality. Instead, we can shape our own destiny and that of our profession by adapting to changed circumstances, integrating the three roles as clinician, manager and informal leader into one professional self-ideal.

Karen Vibeke Mortensen's chapter concentrates on research and classification, a rich field for power struggle. Research is hard work, but unless it also contains aspects of creativity and even play, it becomes lifeless and dull for both the researcher and the audience. She describes some of the special difficulties connected with research in clinical child psychology. A factor which at present has quite a limiting effect on research in this field, is the official diagnostic system, be it ICD-10 or DSM-IV. In spite of their limited character but due to their official status, these systems have an enormous power not only to influence, but to govern and control both assessment and treatment of children as well as research. It is paradoxical that at a time when we know more than ever about the importance of early relationships for the formation of psychopathology, we have chosen diagnostic systems that discard this knowledge and concentrate on superficial symptoms. There is discussion why this is so and also why work with children in general, is in a weaker position than work with adults, a fact which cannot be overlooked. Reasons for this may be rational as well as irrational.

To understand the intricate relationship between power and play can facilitate the ability in both theory and practice, to link these concepts in balanced ways. This may be an ideal that we can strive towards. If pressures from outer reality feel too overwhelming, we may be tempted to withdraw and take refuge in the pleasures of play. At other times, we may take up the fight, but feel that too little space is left for play and consequently suffer from the deterioration of that part of our life. So, one purpose of this book may be an attempt to help us focus our attention on how we can maintain this difficult balance.

CHAPTER ONE

Transformation through play: Living with the traumas of the past

Monica Lanyado

P lay has the power to transform. It can be liberating, aggressive, sad, satisfying, illuminating, angry, anarchic, funny and beautiful. The full range of human emotions and experiences are there. Playing can be the bridge to pleasure, joy and internal freedom. It can also be the bridge to unexplored depths of pain, sadness and violence. The capacity to play is the vehicle which holds these often powerful emotions, within a space where they are not acted out in what might otherwise be destructive ways. When the capacity to play breaks down because the symbolic functioning of the player is overwhelmed due to a weakness in the ability to play which has not fully developed, or an overload of what it is trying to carry, powerful uncontained feelings are set loose.

For example, young children need the watchful eye of an adult to help them when playing otherwise, reality steps in before too long because the "as if" quality has been overstretched, and a battle between soldiers becomes a real fight between two angry, rivalrous toddlers (Segal, 1975). Adults also need boundaries which keep play safe. The *game* of football, which often has the sense of being the present day version of a gladiatorial sport, can readily break down into real fights on and off the pitch, where the idea

1

of *playing a game* has been lost and the reality of the referee and police needs to be brought in to restore some kind of order. Little girls playing mummies and babies come to blows when jealousy and possessiveness as well as bossiness, cannot be held within the imaginative play. Sulks, tantrums and tears reflect their feelings of rejection and fury.

Playing with ideas, whether as a child playing with toys and other children, or as an adult "toying" with thoughts which might lead to new ideas, takes place in what Winnicott has described as an intermediate area of experience, a potential space, often now thought of as a 'transitional space' (Winnicott, 1971). Descriptively, this is the third area of our experience, which is neither fully internal nor external, but paradoxically, both. It is the "both-ness" of the paradox which enables intuitive and spontaneous ideas to surface from the depths of the unconscious, when some of the restraints of reality are removed, because it is "only" playing. Like dreaming, playing "speaks" its own language but is still censored and restricted in many ways.

Observing and witnessing the therapeutic process of children who have been severely deprived and traumatised, has taught me that the gradual emergence of the capacity to play is a very important milestone in their long, slow recovery. If the child or young person leaves therapy with a reasonably robust capacity to play, he or she is much better equipped to face the difficulties of their lives, which are still likely to be many and, at times, severe. The same issues are present when working with adults who have been severely traumatised by war, torture or more "everyday" traumatic losses. Here I am thinking about the capacity to play in the adult sense—of finding as creative a way as possible of living with the dreadful traumas of the past and the difficult realities of the present.

The capacity to play

The ordinary development of a capacity to play takes time. For each of us, this will depend on how we manage to grow the third space that we live in, a transitional space between our unique internal and external realities. The growth of this third space continues throughout life. Playing and the growth of transitional space, are vital contributors to our discovery of who we are and what lies in the depths of our beings, driving as well as helping us to navigate the way we live our lives in good times as well as bad.

In childhood, the development of this space will be dependent on the loving care and attention of an adult who is able to be emotionally available to the growing child in the way that Winnicott describes as enabling the child to be alone "in the presence of someone" (Winnicott, 1958). The therapy of children who have been severely neglected, traumatised and abused shows us what happens when this kind of emotional availability has not been present for the child, the often concomitant lack of protection making the child vulnerable to traumatic experiences. Sadly, many of these traumatic experiences have been within the very relationships that are meant to protect the vulnerable child.

Throughout this paper I will be using the words "living" and "playing" in what I believe is a Winnicottian sense (1971). I put it this way because I am often struck by the many different ways in which Winnicott's writings are interpreted by his readers. It is as if we are all speaking the same language but, at times, with very strong regional accents! So I am going to describe what these terms mean for me, derived from what I have understood from reading Winnicott over the years, from which I learn something new each time.

The question of what we mean by "living" life to the full or being "alive" has been addressed by many psychoanalytic writers probably because so many patients bring the difficulties and pain that they feel because they cannot engage with life and truly "live" it (Bollas, 1987; Casement, 1985; Ogden, 1999; Winnicott, 1971). These patients may often be struggling with the opposite of a sense of living: a sense of internal deadness (Ogden, 1999). The ability to live life to the full is not an easy thing to do. It is a challenge and ultimately an achievement. It is not even clear quite what is meant by this every day phrase.

It has something to do with openness to both the beauties and the hardships of life from which we all have to learn as much as possible. It has something to do with pleasure and happiness and what promotes these at times elusive feelings. It also has something to do with being able to bear the sadness and pain that are inevitable parts of life with fortitude. It is an acceptance that for each one of us, life will dish up a very varied menu of experiences that we all have to learn from, without experiencing each hardship as too much of a narcissistic blow, or each achievement as a confirmation of our omnipotence. It is about reaching for a sense of living a balanced life. It is about finding out who we truly are, our place in, and contribution to, an ever changing world. It is about being able to change as we move through our lives, and not cling to the negativities of the past. It is about letting go of what is no longer relevant in our lives, learning to go with the flow of life, so that we can make space for the new.

Now some thoughts about playing. Playing can be hard work; it can be serious and intense. It is free to go wherever it wants because it lives and breathes in its own space somewhere between the internal and external world, the place Winnicott evocatively describes as the "place where we live"; the intermediate space or transitional space (Winnicott, 1971). Playing is present in ideas, in cultural activity, in relaxation and pleasure. It continues throughout life, in adult games with rules, in sexual games and foreplay, in a sense of humour. It can be both a solitary experience and an interpersonal or group experience. It is an achievement because so many internal and external experiences can disrupt and interfere with its natural course. Playing is an expression of the life force.

Most of our patients, be they child, adolescent or adult, seen individually or in a family or other kind of group, will be more able to play at the end of a reasonably successful therapy than they were at the start. Rather than regarding this as a by-product of the therapeutic process, I now have my therapeutic eyes firmly on my patients' capacity to play as the best indicator of the level of emotional health and resilience in their internal worlds. I am always on the alert for the emergence of new kinds of playfulness in my patients and pay particular attention to them, like a vigilant gardener watching over seedlings that I hope to see grow into big healthy plants.

This paper presents the idea that play is a very powerful vehicle for therapeutic change. Play of the kind illustrated below is "play-with-a-serious-purpose". It is a process which, if it can be facilitated through the therapeutic environment and relationship, reconnects or connects for the first time, the individual with their sense of true self. There are many kinds of play, for example, defensive play, boring play and stuck play which are diversions along the way. Part of the therapist's task is to enable the patient to become more able to recognise these different kinds of play so that when they manage to play creatively, this becomes an experience which can be attended to and become a source of more fulfilled living.

The idea of power in this context relates to the strength of what can be achieved through play. Power, in the sense of power-play within the therapeutic relationship, is likely to obscure the freedom of expression of *either patient and/or therapist* and to be anti-therapeutic. The essence of the approach described below is of the therapist getting alongside the patient, however young or constrained the patient may be, so that therapy is an exploration of the patient's internal world, facilitated by the therapist. Whilst power differentials between therapist and patient may play more or less significant parts in the process, depending on what both *patient and/or therapist* bring to the relationship, too much attention to this dynamic may obscure or inhibit the natural processes of healthy playfulness which are arguably as universal as joy, laughter, tears, anger and sadness. Therapy is thus a joint and, in this respect, equal enterprise.

To illustrate the surprising places to which I believe the capacity to play can take our patients, and us as fellow travellers, I am going to describe my work with Gail. I am grateful to Gail's parents for allowing me to describe aspects of her therapy as an illustration of the way in which play can become transforming.

Clinical example

I am going to summarise most of Gail's therapy and then describe in more detail, a session towards the end of her treatment, when she was trying to wean herself from therapy after 5 years of first twice weekly and then once weekly therapy. What I am trying to describe is the ways in which her transitional space grew and transformed during this time. This account shows how she moved from her early, very high levels of erratic and anxiety driven activity, via a very active playful period, to a remarkably meditative and "still" place by the time she felt ready to try to cope with her life without therapy.

Gail started psychoanalytic psychotherapy when she was twelve years old, after a period of art therapy which she had used very positively. She had been adopted when she was seven years old, having been abandoned by her mother when she was five years old.

She had been born with a mild syndrome which meant that she had some slight physical abnormalities in addition to the possibility that she would have permanent learning difficulties. The most significant feature of her early life was that both of her birth parents were profoundly deaf, whilst she was able to hear quite normally. Her birth parents had also had very difficult childhoods with her father diagnosed as having a personality disorder. It was because of his violence towards Gail's mother that she walked out of the marriage when Gail was eighteen months old. Gail had probably witnessed many frightening arguments and was neglected in many ways but it is unlikely that she was physically or sexually abused.

The current social policy in the UK around helping such children makes every effort to place these children in families rather than children's homes. Consequently, after some brief and unsuccessful attempts before she was five to keep her in her birth family, she was placed with first one and then another foster family, before her adoptive family were found when she was seven years old.

The early days of Gail's therapy were characterised by her impulsivity and inability to stay with any play theme for more than a few minutes. She was, like many other children who have suffered this kind of early history, unpredictable and quixotic (Cleve, 2004; Edwards, 2000; Hindle, 2000). I always felt very on edge and hyper-alert when with her as I had no idea what she might do next such as rush out of the room, insist on playing in the hallway instead of in the therapy room, shutting me out of the therapy room or re-arranging all the furniture in the room. This kind of difficulty around holding the boundaries of the therapy will be very familiar to those working with severely traumatised and deprived children. Thankfully, she was never physically aggressive towards me although she could often be rude and disdainful, flouncing out of the room or ignoring me as if I was totally worthless. She was extremely difficult for her adoptive parents to live with hence the referral. They had regular therapeutic support throughout her treatment.

Playful interpretation

Gradually, Gail became able to listen a little bit more to the few comments and interpretations that I managed to make. This came about as the result of what I came to think of as "playful interpretations" which, rather like someone trying to spoon-feed a reluctant baby, I managed to persuade her to take in by being "playfully present" for her whilst actually offering her something very serious. This was always a very delicate dance between us as I needed to be alert to when she was playfully available and then find a way of engaging her with what I wanted to say to her. This is the kind of "therapeutic seedling" I am trying to illustrate that I referred to earlier which can carry a great potential for growth.

For example, for a long while when I started to try to talk more seriously to her about our relationship by making a transference interpretation, or when I tried to verbalise something that might have been helpful for her to think about that had become evident from her fragments of play, she would often simply cover her ears, turn her back or walk out of the room. I eventually decided that I might get further if she was able to feel more in control of the alarming things which she felt came out of my mouth, and playfully asked her if I could say something "very small" about what was happening at a particular moment. She agreed but in her typically controlling way said, rather warily, but also slightly playfully, "How small?" I spontaneously put out my parted hands in front of me, indicating a short length of words, at which she smiled faintly and her eyes twinkled slightly as she said, "Okay then but no more than that". For a considerable time, I prefaced much of what I wanted to say with this question and it provided a communication bridge between us. There were plenty of times when she refused my requests but, just as with my parallel of the feeding of a reluctant baby, I would persevere as far as seemed non-forceful and try again in some other way, later in the session.

This paved the way for us to play lengthy role-playing games which continued from one session to the next. Whilst I followed her lead in these games, my focus was much more often on enabling her to keep playing, rather than interpreting the content of the play. By this point, I had realised that it was the playing itself, as a medium of communication of her deepest concerns that I wanted to facilitate. I rarely linked the content of her play with her past life as this was still too overwhelming for her and likely to disrupt the play which I felt was so healing for her. It was the actual experience of playing, both within therapy and increasingly in her everyday life that I felt was transforming her ability to communicate what she was living with in her inner world.

Whilst I did not interpret the play, I was always paying very close attention to it and "listening" very carefully to what she was trying to communicate while trying to make some sense of it in my own mind. In this respect, I was being the person who she was "alone in the presence of" as she played (see Lanyado, 2004 for a fuller discussion of this idea). The fact that Gail's birth parents were both deaf whilst she had normal hearing was a constant yet easily overlooked factor in all our communications. It was as if this very difficult reality soaked into everything that took place between us, probably most profoundly in the ways that I felt that I listened to her with my *total being*. I felt utterly absorbed in trying to understand what she was trying to communicate, even though I often had to accept that I really had not understood at all. This may well have been a vivid re-experiencing in the transference-countertransference relationship because of the communication difficulties that are inevitable in parent-child relationships where the child has normal hearing and the parents are deaf. For these relationships to work one can imagine that other channels of communication need to be intensified and turned to full volume; it was this that must have been so hard for her birth parents to manage.

Play, as a vital form of communication, created the pathway for the transformations that Gail was able to make in her life. Her ability to concentrate started to grow and this became evident in her improved schoolwork which she shyly let me see during what at times, felt like endless varieties of games of schools. Other games involved wafer thin enactments of her birth mother's abandonment of her, in which she was able to express some of her outrage that a mother could behave like this towards her daughter. However, only rarely was I allowed to relate these games to her own experience and when this did happen, it was mostly at her instigation. This stage of therapy is discussed in more detail elsewhere (Lanyado, 2006).

Starting to live with the trauma of the past

Approximately two and a half years into her therapy, when she was close to fifteen years old, things started to change and we became more able to talk about what had happened to her. She was emotionally much stronger by then and, of her own accord, suddenly decided to bring her Life Story Book to the sessions, eventually leaving it in my safe keeping for us to look at together, over roughly the next two years. This was one of the spontaneous ideas which I believe emerged from her growing transitional space. All children in the UK who have been moved from their birth families have a Life Story Book, compiled by social workers and foster carers, containing the most important information about their birth families and foster families. This book is often the heartbreaking story of their life, sometimes in a sanitised form, at other times in a horribly, matter-of-fact form.

We spent a great deal of time pouring over the photos of Gail with her birth family, foster families and the early days with her adoptive family. The information was contained in a loose leaf file and many sessions were spent with her arranging and then re-arranging the pages as she tried to find some way of making sense of all of it. During this period of her therapy, I realise in retrospect that I spent a great deal of time quietly sitting with her as she searched the pages with great concentration for clues about herself and who she was. I mused and wondered to myself about a young life that had become fragmented in this dreadful way and about her loneliness and vulnerability when she had no permanent family that cared for her. Often, although I said very little, I felt tremendously sad and thought that I was starting to hold some of the feelings of painful loss, as well as the beginnings of some mourning, that Gail was not yet ready to feel inside herself.

There was a quiet determination about Gail as she did this important and painful work. She seemed to have some bearings on what she needed to sort out within herself and, in her own way persisted with this, despite the anger that it raised in her. Although she was now fifteen, she still spent a good deal of time playing in her sessions. However, many sessions were spent with her quietly drawing in an abstract design sort of way, as she discovered that she had some artistic ability in the midst of her disappointment, and at times her despair, with her otherwise limited intellectual abilities. By this point, I no longer felt hyper-alert during the sessions and was able to sit and think about what was happening in a very focused way. I hardly ever felt bored or unable to think because of any attacks on thinking that originated in Gail. I felt able to truly listen to her.

The "ending" stage of therapy

It was very difficult to decide when it would be most appropriate to bring Gail's therapy to a close. Her parents, Gail and I eventually decided that we should meet until she had had one term in a college which offered courses for youngsters with special educational difficulties. By the time we made this decision, six months before the suggested ending, she was in touch with some more ordinary adolescent needs for independence and told me rather archly that I would have to let her go at some point as she couldn't carry on coming to see me for ever! At the same time she was able to say that she was rather worried about managing without therapy altogether, so we decided that when her once weekly sessions came to an end, we would meet roughly every month during school term time for as long as she wanted. This kind of post-therapy contact is not unusual when working with children and families such as these. It provides a self-weaning opportunity for a child who has previously suffered abandonment in reality by the adults who should have protected and cared for them. It was important for Gail to feel that she could leave me in her own time and at her own pace.

Gail rose to the challenge of going to college and took what felt like a developmental leap into delayed, early-adolescent behaviour. Before this, at the age of sixteen, she was still very much a late latency-type child, showing limited signs of adolescent behaviour. She was, however, becoming more and more her own more "rounded" self, able to love, be angry and then repair where she had made mistakes. She was a "character", able to express many good qualities such as honesty, trustworthiness, gratitude and perseverance, mixed up with the inevitable scars of her early childhood. Now she chatted in the session about clothes, pop groups and romantic crushes on boys. She took great care about her appearance and looked attractive and feminine without being inappropriately sexualised. She developed her own version of street credibility, complete with mobile phone, heavy irony and sarcasm, and struggled generally to hold her own at college amongst her group of similarly struggling contemporaries.

Gail shared her distress with me as she realised more and more how different she and her "special" group were from the mainstream college kids. She longed to be ordinary but knew that she was not the same as them and would always feel on the outside of that teenage world. Her anger about this was added to her anger about being neglected and abandoned by her mother and not having had a permanent secure and loving home until she was seven years old. She felt she had been dealt a very bad hand of cards in life's game. She knew that she belonged more with the "special" group, but this meant having to realistically accept her limitations living in the ordinary world, something which was naturally very hard for her. She surprised me again by doggedly and quite maturely making great efforts to take on many of the more ordinary adolescent issues of identity which, for her, included trying to make some sense of who her mother had been as a person and why she should still at times feel such a longing to see her, despite her ongoing fury with her.

All of this, she communicated with her characteristic bluntness. Throughout her struggles, she was also touchingly able to express to me her gratitude and love for her adoptive parents, how they had changed her life and for all they continued to give to her. This demonstrated a capacity to tolerate many paradoxes in her life in a manner that did not keep seeking false answers to her life's difficulties. It was harder for her to show this appreciation directly to her adoptive parents and she could still be very moody and angry with them. But there were other times when she could be unequivocal and movingly loving about how much they meant to her and how she felt they had saved her life.

The last two months of her therapy further illustrated the transformation that had been taking place in her during all the quiet times that followed the liveliness of her earlier playfulness. This process of transformation originated in her ability to play and developed into a growing ability to *live* what was still a difficult life, as she became increasingly aware of the limitations of her intellectual abilities as well as the scars of the past traumas. I am postulating that, through the earlier phase of her active playing, she developed the medium of the *capacity to play* in the transitional space that grew both within her and between us. This in turn enabled her to have some very creative ideas about what might help her, such as her unusual use of her Life Story Book in our sessions.

In her new teenage mode, at the age of seventeen, Gail tended to communicate for the whole session without toys or drawing materials. Strikingly, she now often, but not always, came into the room and immediately went to the couch, carefully rearranging the cushions into what I always thought of as "adult" mode before lying down on the couch as an adolescent or adult patient would. It is highly unlikely that she had any knowledge that this was the way adult and late adolescent patients used the couch. Sometimes she would chatter away to me as if I was one of her new college friends. At other times, she would be moodily quiet and verbally uncommunicative. Then there were some sessions in which she again astonished me, with her clear insight into the difficulties of her current life; of trying to grow up and become more independent, in a realistic way.

The pressure of therapy coming to an end added to this, and she was able to talk about how she wanted a boyfriend who would value her and look after her. She knew that she needed looking after and was able to look at the boys who were showing interest in her and try to assess how caring they were able to be towards her. This was her most important criterion for their suitability as a boyfriend and indicated how much she had gained and internalised from having an adoptive father who looked after and cared for her. When we explored this a bit more, she was very clear that she knew that she would find it hard to live independently as an adult, and would need some form of looking after by someone other than her parents. They were getting older and with great difficulty she was able to say 'what will happen to me when they die?'

She could understand that this connected to her fears of how she would cope without me and, for the first time, was clearly thinking about not only her current life situation but also her future. At times like these she was able to think deeply and through what she said, as well as some very sad, long and rather forlorn prolonged eye contact with me, powerfully conveyed the pain and depression that she was now managing to contain within her a good deal of the time. This was a much more mature kind of adolescent development in which she was wondering about what life had in store for her.

I want to give a more detailed account of one of her last sessions, which is what prompted me to write this paper as I found it so extraordinary.

Clinical material

Gail came into the room and went straight to the couch, re-arranging the cushions to make herself comfortable before lying down. I sat opposite to her in what was my usual chair, which resulted in us facing each other. She said "What? ... ." in an aggressive, challenging way, as if feeling persecuted by my looking at her; a familiar theme. I did not rise to this and just remained quiet. As if to excuse herself for being rude she said, "I'm just tired", in a stroppy, adolescent-ish way. She then chatted inconsequentially about a broken nail, the dark winter night, how cold it was and the fact that I had the curtains closed and the lights on. She relaxed on the couch, curling up in a loose foetal position in which I couldn't see her face, and then became quiet.

After a while I made a comment which was intended to try to help her to talk if she wished to. She told me that she didn't want to talk and then spent the rest of the session—forty minutes—amazingly still and quiet in this same loose, foetal position, but alert and awake. She felt very present and as had so often been my experience when I had been quietly with her in the past, I felt free to think about and experience the ebb and flow of what this extraordinarily still experience with her could be about.

It felt as if she had entered a quiet, unpersecuted space and I was being allowed to follow her into it, feeling separate but intensely "present". The space did not feel sad, depressed or angry. Its strongest quality was its intense stillness. At times, it felt as if I was a mother sitting quietly with her baby, not wanting to move in case I disturbed her. But as I became more and more aware of the stillness itself, I was amazed to realise that what I was most aware of was how much the stillness in Gail was like a meditative state. This rather stunned me as I have become increasingly interested in the parallels and connections between meditative states and practices, and the kind of quiet "holding" in a Winnicottian sense that often takes place in therapy.

I found myself thinking of all the different kinds of silence and quietness we had experienced together during her therapy and marvelled at how we had reached this place after all the activity and impulsiveness of the first few years of her therapy. I did not say any of this to her, not wanting to disrupt the precious state of mind she seemed to be in.

For a while I tried to be as still as she was but realised that I was not able to do this despite having meditated in this way for many years. This only served to emphasise to me how extraordinary it was that she was able to stay in this "place" for as long as she was. As we got closer to the end of the session, I felt that I wanted to say something about what was happening and commented on how different this stillness was from other times we had been quietly together. It seemed to be helping her to feel some peace inside herself, and it seemed to be good for her. Within myself, I realised that what she seemed to be absorbing deeply from me, under the pressure of weekly therapy coming to an end, was that part of me that values these still, meditative states and sees them as being deeply transforming and healing. It was an unconscious identification with a part of me that I had not realised she had somehow perceived.

Without feeling that my words would disrupt the state she was in, I was able to say to her that her ability to reach this stillness was something that would stay with her when she stopped coming to see me each week, and that it was a place within her that she could go to when things were hard, that would offer her some peace of mind. It was a link between us and could also be a place of internal refuge to her when she needed it. The session ended, feeling like a combination of a therapy session and meditation practice. I told her that we had a few more minutes and at first she jumped up from her position on the couch. However, I said that there was no rush and she could just slowly emerge and get up from the couch when she was ready, which she then did. The sense of stillness remained with her as she left the session.

Her next session was very similar to this, but her last session was much more defensive again as she spent much of the time shutting me out. The memories of other goodbyes, to her birth mother and foster parents, still remained too alive for her not to be rather defensive when faced with the reality of the parting. At the time of writing this paper, Gail continues to see me approximately once a month.

Discussion

Writing about a patient whose therapy is ongoing is always a bit of a risk as it is true to say that, more than anything, only time will tell if the therapy has been helpful or not. But there is also the advantage that writing and reflecting on therapy as it happens, makes it a very alive experience and can in itself nourish and stimulate thought about the patient in a fruitful way. Extending Parsons' thinking about the analyst's countertransference to the psychoanalytic process, I would add that the process of writing about a patient can be seen as part of the counter-transference processing of the patient's and therapist's work together. I see this writing as blending into the therapeutic process as a whole (Parsons, 2006).

When I first wrote about my work with Gail, I wanted to understand more about what I saw as a deliberate change in my technique and why it seemed to be taking the therapeutic process forward (Lanyado, 2006). I was already very aware of how important it was to facilitate playing in my patients, as well as very aware of how difficult this could be for many patients who could not authentically start to play or have an idea. What I learnt with Gail was that it was helpful for the playful part of me to be much more present in the room with this kind of patient than it was with patients who were already able to play to some measure.

My understanding of behaving in a "professional" manner before this time, meant that I felt I should leave this part of me "outside the consulting room door". But as I have come to appreciate how important it is for the therapeutic process, for the therapist to be "present" in the room, I now re-define this task as being about how the therapist can be fully present as a whole person whilst trying very hard not to impinge with his or her ego-driven needs on the patient in the room. When this is the *intention*, the therapist is more able to use her whole Self, in a very personal way, to enter into the "overlap of two areas of playing, that of the patient and that of the therapist" (Winnicott, 1971, p. 44). I emphasise "intention" as this is something to strive towards, another kind of therapeutic self-disciplining in the therapist's self-awareness, alongside the other guiding principles of good practice, as opposed to an absolutely attainable state of mind.

Gail always had the capacity to surprise me with her sudden insights and growth spurts. These would seem to come out of the blue but, in reality, I now realise that they came *out of the depths* of her being. There was something about the qualities of the overlap of our play (transitional) spaces, that we were able to reach during the quieter times of her therapy, which I now think related to the many ways in which I tried to listen to her with "my whole being" (Fransman, 2006). This may have enabled these aspects of her Self to reach the surface. This quietness was not an externally observable quietness, particularly during the very playful period of her therapy, that is physically, there would often be a lot of noise during the session. It probably had more to do with my efforts to be as intensely receptive as possible to all that was happening and the fact that she did not feel threatened by this when she entered the transitional space that we created between us. It is very important, as it is still clear from the session I have described in more detail, that she could often feel very persecuted by a simple look from me. But if I held my internally quiet and receptive stance, she could enter the transitional experience with me and allow something unexpected to happen. My internal quietness and resolve seemed to enable her to cross this threshold and possibly even attracted her towards it. Maybe it was like some kind of 'invitation to the dance' which she gradually became drawn towards.

So far in this paper, I have been descriptive giving what I hope is a plausible and authentic account of what took place between us. There are two very different ways of thinking about what happened which I think deeply resonate and converge with what I have described and which I think provide further support for the validity of my hypothesis.

Firstly, Schore's writings about relational trauma and how relationships can also help to reduce the high stress hormone, cortisol, levels in the brain, resulting from persistent early traumatisation and neglect, provide an exciting parallel scientific universe to the experiential universe I have described so far (Schore, 2003).

What we seem to now understand, is how impossible and indeed simplistic it is to try to separate mind, brain, body and human experience. We are learning to live with this complexity. (For accessible accounts of the impact of new understandings in neurophysiology relevant to traumatised children, see Gerhardt, 2004, and Music, 2006). Children like Gail who have been so consistently traumatised during the vital stages of early brain development, during late pregnancy and the first two years of life, have literally become "wired" neurologically to react with the full range of the fight-flight nervous and physiological responses to what to other people would be imperceptible threats. Their neural networks have literally been selectively "pruned" and shaped by their traumatic and terrifying experiences and this in turn, affects their whole biochemistry and physiology, as they become tense and ready for action at the least perceived threat to their safety (Perry et al., 1995).

By contrast, children who started their lives in calm, loving relationships will have brains that have been bathed in calming chemicals, opiates and hormones. Their cortisol levels will be low and their whole body will be more relaxed and not constantly at risk of being flooded by adrenaline, priming them for fight or flight responses. Schore argues that positive loving communications from the carer to the infant trigger positive biochemical responses in the infant's body. These in turn, determine which neuronal pathways are established, used and reinforced in the infant's brain, as well as synchronising the physiological processes within the infant and carer's bodies at the time. For example, during ordinary loving holding and touching of the baby, the mother's "autonomic nervous system in effect communicates with her baby's nervous system, soothing it through touch" (Gerhardt, 2004, p. 40).

Whilst this process is most potent during infancy and very early childhood, if there were not other opportunities throughout life for the damage done to the brain and body to be corrected, we would never see any recovery at all from early trauma, and we know that this is not the case. However, as all who work with traumatised patients recognise, it is enormously difficult for the patient to feel less anxious or to become less vulnerable to the old triggers that produce emotional and physical fear and panic responses. Realistically, we need to think in terms of partial recovery. Therapy is one of the routes into this process and Gail's therapy illustrates this in her move from hyper-reactivity and hyper-alertness at the start of therapy, through to her extraordinary stillness in the session described above.

Following Schore's conceptions, one could postulate that my "calming" body and brain were communicating with her body and brain during the times when we "overlapped" in the transitional space we had created between us. How this communication crosses the 'ether' between one body and another remains a mystery which we continue to try to understand. But it is not really that far removed from the extraordinary ways in which, for example, mobile phones enable us speak to someone at the other end of the country by simply putting an elegant piece of plastic and metal to our ears. We cannot see the passage of energy between us, but we observe and experience its power.

Now for the second resonance with my hypothesis which some may find more surprising. This relates to thoughts about meditative states which may occur in the therapist's or analyst's mind during a session, and how these relate to other calming, holding and containing states of mind. It is good to see that meditative, spiritual and religious experiences have come in from the psychoanalytic cold over the past fifteen years or so, culminating in the recent publication of the thoughtful collection of papers, *Psychoanalysis and Religion in the 21st Century* (Black, 2006). It seems that this area of human experience can now legitimately be considered alongside other qualities of the therapist/analyst's mind, as it affects the patient both during and outside sessions.

An ongoing and fascinating collaboration and discussion between very experienced Buddhist monks, including the Dalai Lama and leading neuroscientists, has lead to a series of experiments in which brain activity during meditation is being measured using EEGs and fMRI scans. Published findings indicate that meditation can bring both immediate and long term changes in brain activity, associated with feelings of well-being which we, as clinicians, might associate with emotional recovery or healing. (For a detailed description of this research and references see Ricard, 2007, chapter 16.) In the UK, meditation is increasingly recommended as a means of lowering stress levels.

This suggests an intriguing convergence between clinical experience, neuroscientific research, and very ancient meditative practices that have stood the test of time over thousands of years. These very different ways of thinking about human behaviour all suggest that quietness and stillness are not only beneficial to ordinary well being, but may also be healing. It is this kind of convergence that can help us as clinicians to make choices about what kind of technique is valid and appropriate with our patients, depending on their individual needs.

In addition, it is helpful to note that meditational practices are embedded in a tradition of wisdom and thought which has much to offer contemporary psychoanalytic thought (for example, see Parsons, 2000). For example, one of the aims of some forms of meditation is to "still the mind". The idea that Gail's sudden insights arose spontaneously from the depths of her being, as a result of a form of stillness, is expressed very beautifully in the Tao Te Ching, written approximately 2,500 years ago. In one of the many chapters which to me, resonate profoundly with our work, Lao Tzu, beautifully translated by Stephen Mitchell, writes

> Do you have the patience to wait
> Till your mud settles and the water is clear?
> Can you remain unmoving
> until the right action arises by itself?
> (Lao Tzu, tr. Stephen Mitchell, chapter 15)

These ancient teachings are advocating meditational practices which still the mind as a means of gaining clarity and enabling new ideas to emerge from the depths. When Gail spontaneously demonstrated an ability to reach towards this stillness, I was able to connect this with a particular aspect of what has probably become a natural part of the way I am when I am quiet. The fact that Gail might have unconsciously identified with this, particularly under the pressure of ending her weekly sessions with me, was something which had not occurred to me.

For many years I have meditated at the start of the day, for my own personal reasons, as well as to help me to be in a calm and receptive internal state in order to be able to be as undefended as possible when with my patients. This has helped me significantly, personally and professionally, as I have come to know how hard it is to still the mind during meditation, let alone during everyday life. This is why it is so necessary to practice meditation. There is no end point. Nina Coltart wrote and talked in interviews with Molino in 1997 and 1998, about her experiences of the links between psychoanalysis, meditation and Buddhism (Molino, 1997 and 1998). She has this to say about meditation.

"One of its richest fruits can be a deepening quality which is essential for the good-enough practice of psychoanalysis: I refer to something for which there is no one exact word, but it has to do with patience, with waiting, with 'negative capability' which, inseparably linked with the continued exercise of bare attention, create the deepest atmosphere in which the analysis takes place. The more one actually just attends and the less one actually *thinks* during an analytical session, the more open one is to learning to trust the intuition that arises from the less rational and cognitive parts of the self, and the more open one is to a full and direct apprehension of the patient and of what is actually going on .... The discipline of meditation practice enhances the discipline of one's contribution to an analytic session which sometimes is, in fact, itself almost indistinguishable from a form of meditation" (Coltart, 1992, pp. 173–174, original italics).

Having started this paper and Gail's treatment with thoughts about the importance of facilitating her *capacity* to play, it is rather startling to see where we have ended up. Playing can transform experience in totally unexpected ways. This is the journey of potentiality and discovery that we embark on with every one of our patients.

DISCUSSION

The power of play—a comment on Monica Lanyado's article: 'Transformation through play: Living with the traumas of the past'

Liselotte Grünbaum

My first thought after reading Monica Lanyado's contribution, was that this enjoyable and wise article speaks for itself and provides such an inspiring space for reflection for any child psychotherapist no matter what his or her orientation, that really, it needs no comment. Monica Lanyado gives us a delightful account of the psychotherapeutic process with a severely deprived and traumatised adolescent and follows this up with a thoughtful discussion of how to understand the development that took place.

Lanyado provides a vivid picture of the atmosphere and process in the psychoanalytic playroom. She allows us to have a real look into the specific character of the therapeutic relationship arising from a background of mental pain and damage relating to an early experience of comprehensive deprivation and trauma. Thus the therapeutic journey takes us from confusion, aggressive contempt and despair, through a playful intermediate space and, as the end of therapy is approaching, finally to utter silence, in addition to hope for a better future with some capacity for thoughtful mourning and realistic self appraisal.

From a position rooted in the Independent tradition, the Winnicottian idea of play as the major vehicle in development permeates Lanyado's work in general, as well as this article (Lanyado, 2004;

21

Lanyado & Horne, 2006). She has decisively developed the richness of the concept of therapeutic neutrality by adding to it *the playful presence of the therapist*, a concept that has become a most useful tool for child psychotherapists belonging to diverse theoretical traditions, working with troubled and disturbed children.

As pointed out by Barnett (2006), the theoretical stance of the Independent tradition, may be best summed up with the statement "evaluate and respect ideas for their use and truth value no matter whence they come"[1] (p. xi). This stance has a number of advantages, as amply evidenced in Lanyado's article, by the strength of a flexible point of view that allows for a willingness to experiment with new ideas and techniques, trying to adapt these to the perceived needs of the patients. Nevertheless, this broadness of mind may have its price, as the absence of a unified system of thought may hinder the powerful, qualitative development that stems from contrasting, conflicting points of view.

Accordingly, in this comment, I will do my best from a Kleinian stance, to raise questions that hopefully will lead to a fruitful conflict between differing theoretical points of view. There are some questions implicit in the text which Lanyado offers answers to. My suggestion is not to take the answers for granted; the four questions given below are amongst others that deserve to be pondered over by the reader:

1. The role of play in the development generated by child psychotherapy? Related to this, why Gail's newly acquired capacity to play verbally with ideas, thoughts and feelings had to break down so completely before the therapy could come to an end?
2. When, and no less how, can the painful feelings relating to the past be linked verbally to the transference relationship?
3. When and how to plan for a proper ending in child psychotherapy?
4. Last but not least, how can we conceive of a cross-discipline explanation for the events of a psychoanalytic psychotherapy process, in which widely differing schools of thought such as psychoanalysis, neuroscience and the meditation tradition are combined?

---

[1]Cited from Barnett, who cites Rayner, E. (1990): *The Independent Mind in British Psychoanalysis*. London: Free Association Books.

It is outside the scope and space of this short comment to give an adequate elucidation of the questions therefore, I will not try to do this. I will however, concentrate my efforts on the first and the last questions, namely, the role of play in child psychotherapy and how to combine different schools of thought.

The role of play in psychotherapy

In the prelude to the clinical case, Lanyado herself presents a truly Winnicottian point of view, namely, what really works in getting Gail's development started and eventually helps her growing ability to live, is the offer of an intermediate space with possibilities for development through play. Her description makes a convincing case for the development of a capacity to play being a major developmental step for Gail. At a technical level, it is impressive to follow the creative child therapist as she manages to hold the situation, while a confused and terrified youngster struggles to keep in control. Thus Lanyado gently finds a playful way for the child, by letting Gail set limits to words, while at the same time patiently keeping up a clear and unfaltering therapeutic intention to offer at least some verbally expressed understanding.

However, thinking about the mechanisms involved in the process of change, play is not the sole possible factor to consider. A quest for power is present in the deprived child's need to keep in control, and the creative therapist finds a benign way to keep in power by taking "meta-control" of the relationship. At a technical level, Lanyado's descriptions of how she playfully took control over her own language to enable the child to feel in control, has a distinct similarity to Fred Pine's descriptions of ego supportive work with borderline adolescents, through the patient offering of a stable setting and a relationship in which any interpretation is phrased in an ego-supporting way, with due respect for the survival strategies of the child (Pine, 1985).

From a contemporary Kleinian point of view, a third way to understand the development of Gail is possible. Behind both the development of an intermediate space in the therapeutic relationship and Gail's growing ability to play, may lie the introjection of a containing relationship and, through this, the development of the ability for symbolic functioning; a development of the fundamental mental apparatus of Gail's mind. At the theoretical level, this relates to Bion's model of container-contained as a condition for the development of a mentalising mind. Thus it is possible that Gail's growing ability to play, to understand herself and to think reflectively, may be contingent on the introjection of the relationship to a therapist unfaltering in her wish to mirror and relate to Gail's feelings and thoughts in the here and now (Bion, 1970; Fonagy et al., 2002).

As mentioned, further questions relate to if, when and no less, how to make the link verbally between painful feelings relating to the past and the transference relationship. I was very moved by Lanyado's patience in enduring what must have felt like an endless transference enactment of the being together with non-hearing objects. Eventually, her persistent wish to understand without rushing the child was rewarded as Gail, of her own accord, brought the scattered pieces of her past into the verbal therapeutic dialogue. No doubt readers will want to compare this way of working with their own experience of how best to relate to a patient's experience of past deprivations and traumas.

Why the silence?

Irrespective of the preferred psychoanalytic vantage point, an adequate explanation of Gail's development must also be able to account for the surprising fact that Gail's newly acquired capacity to play verbally with ideas, thoughts and feelings, had to break down so completely before the therapy could reach an ending.

On the one hand, in the carefully reported session, the therapist experienced a peaceful feeling of quiet holding. She suggests herself that the persecuted part of Gail is calmed and contained by the quiet and receptive stance of the therapist, thus enabling her to enter a transitional space in deep identification with the inner resources of the therapist. To follow this thought, Gail's profoundly silent state may be about an urgent need to let go of a confused part of the infantile self, whose only way to keep alive was by hanging desperately and closely on to shifting moods and ways of not-hearing, edgy objects.

However, it is my job to raise questions, thereby opening the analysis to a range of different considerations. At the very beginning of the session, Gail's persecuted, quite aggressive "what" is followed by a retreat that gives us a glimpse of the deprived child's characteristic way of seeking care through worries about hurts and cold. Might it be that Gail, confronted with the anxiety about parting, needs very much to forget the long, dark winter nights out in the cold that is the past and the future without regular therapy? From this perspective, could the peaceful, but also wide-awake silence be about seeking shelter and comfort in the secluded, well-lit therapeutic space? In this light, one may ponder if the silence contains certain traces of an anxious, hearing baby seeking a soothing feeling of unbroken, harmonious relatedness to a deaf mother.

On playing with interdisciplinary explanations—is it play or power play?

The described development of Gail is impressive, especially taking into consideration the objective features of the case, namely Gail's age both at adoption, 7 years, and at the start of therapy, 12 years, the limitations to her learning capacities and her early, severe, and recurrent experiences of deprivation and traumatisation. We know both from psychotherapy research and from child psychological studies of early deprivation and adoption, that the older and more damaged the child in question has become, the more difficult it is to achieve change either through psychotherapy or through better environmental provision (Kennedy, 2004; O'Connor et al., 1999; Rutter, 1999; Target & Fonagy, 1994).

Lanyado courageously looks at how the causal mechanisms in this development may be understood from a perspective outside psychoanalytic theory itself. She generously offers two widely different frames of reference, namely neuroscience and meditation. The first perspective is of modern neuroscience: Schore's suggestion that early relational trauma due to neglect and abuse, resulting in high stress levels and changes in neuronal pathways, will influence the development of the infant's brain and consequently lead to difficulties in affect regulation and adaptation (Schore, 2003). This explanation leaves space for the hypothesis that a better relational experience in later childhood may bring about partial recovery. Indeed, as demonstrated by Lanyado, child psychotherapy may be thought of as a specific form of such a relational experience, one in which the two participants become intensely involved in each other's minds.

The second perspective originates in the tradition of meditation practices: the ancient experience of letting go of conscious thought and preoccupation to enter an inner state of quietness which has the potential to heal the troubled mind. This viewpoint may also be linked to a psychoanalytic perspective of change in that the crucial factor seems to be the therapist's patience in waiting and staying receptive. Again, I cannot but think of Bion (1970), who would interpret this as the therapist's negative capability to attend and stay attentive while not actually thinking or reaching out for conscious understanding or, to follow Lanyado herself, as the ability to create a wordless, transitional space in which peaceful aloneness can take place[2].

In our time, it has become popular to offer cross-disciplinary explanations for what happens in the therapeutic process. While quite aware of the disadvantage of isolation from other scientific traditions to the psychoanalytic discourse, I cannot but help remembering the recurrent warning of a teacher of statistics who used to remind his students that before accepting a given causal explanation, one has to understand which kind of "why-question" is answered by the explanation. We have to think about whether or not the explanations given from the neuroscientific, meditational and psychoanalytic point of view can be epistemologically compared, or if it is rather like trying to compare the height of the Eifel Tower with the loudness of a peal of thunder. Neuroscience and meditation have widely differing epistemological roots and both are related to disciplines outside the field of psychoanalytic theory itself. Thus, we may think about how to compare and reconcile these three diverse theoretical platforms. One view could be that the three perspectives are related to each other by a mutual concern regarding how the mind develops and may be healed.

---

[2]It would take me too far off the path to follow this thought through, however, I must mention that in "The Borderline Concept", Green (1977) compared Winnicott's concept "the capacity to be alone", Bion's concept "negative capability", Lacan's concept "absence" and reached the conclusion that problems relating to aloneness (separation) and reunion is a recurrent theme in development—and especially poignant in the borderline existence because of an inability to answer either yes or no to the absence of the object.

CHAPTER TWO

Has play the power to change group and patients in group analysis?

Peter Ramsing

Clinical example

> *In a group of women recovering from anorexia nervosa, one of the participants, Ms M, is evaluating her first year in the group. She eats normally and is of normal weight, but she misses being thin. She says that longing to be thin again is like unrequited love. She continues talking. One of the therapists returns to the association between unrequited love and her anorexia, and it starts a further discussion with lively participation from the rest of the group. Themes such as the following are discussed: If you are going to leave a lover, you have to mourn. It is difficult if he does not want you any longer or has found another (thin?) girl. Unrequited love restricts your life if you are not setting yourself free from the relationship.*

Time will tell if Ms M can use this image on her way to a full recovery but in the group, it was obvious that the discussion changed from a matter-of-fact discussion to a playing mode, in pretending that Ms M's anorexia was a former lover.

It is a commonly held opinion that only children play, but as the example above illustrates, this idea is based on a very limited conception of play and playing. A Dutch cultural historian, Johan Huizinga (1963), sees play as universal and argues in his book *Homo Ludens* (*Man the Player*) that *play is part of creating culture* and not the other way around. A quote from his book seems pertinent:

> "Play is a voluntary activity or occupation, executed within certain fixed limits of time and place, according to rules freely accepted, but absolutely binding, having its aim in itself and accompanied by a feeling of tension, joy and the consciousness that it is "different" from "ordinary life". Thus defined, the concept seemed capable of embracing everything we call "play" in animals, children and grown-ups: games of strength and skill, inventing games, guessing games, games of chance, exhibitions and performances of all kinds. We ventured to call the category "play" one of the most fundamental in life" (1963, p. 28).

In his book, Huizinga gives examples from history of how "the two ever-recurrent forms in which *civilization grows in and as play* are the sacred performance and the festal contest" (1963, p. 48). Seen in this way, play has an archaic dimension for Man and Culture.

Winnicott (1971) also saw play as fundamental:

> "*It is play that is universal* and that belongs to health: playing facilitates growth and therefore health; playing leads into group relationships; playing can be a form of communication in psychotherapy; and, lastly, psychoanalysis has been developed as a highly specialized form of playing in the service of communication with oneself and others. The natural thing is playing and the highly sophisticated twentieth century phenomenon is psychoanalysis" (1971, p. 48).

André Green (2005) states that there is no culture without play and that there are no periods of history from which play has been absent. He says:

> "My conclusion, therefore, is that play, this universal activity, belongs to an innate attribute of the mind that takes different shapes, not only in various groups, but also for different individuals" (2005, p. 11).

Mook (1998) writes about imaginative play in child psychotherapy, linking up with Merleau-Ponty's philosophy and his phenomenology of structure. Seen in this way, imaginative play exemplifies human order, enabling the child to create and re-create his own meanings in an embodied way. This, in turn, changes the child's experience and potentially leads to surprising insights and discoveries relevant to their life-world. Herein lays the central value of imaginative play and its promise to facilitate change and healing in a therapeutic context. In Mook's own words:

> "For play evokes a primordial experience of ourselves and exhibits par excellence what it means to be a lived body in the world" (1998, p. 236).

This perspective on play is similar to Winnicott's way of describing play. He describes transitional phenomena as part of play. Transitional phenomena are located neither in inner nor in outer reality:

> "*Playing has a place and a time.* It is not *inside* by any use of the word (and it is unfortunately true that the word inside has very many and various uses in the psychoanalytic discussion). Nor is it *outside,* that is to say, it is not part of the repudiated world, the not-me, that which the individual has decided to recognize (with whatever difficulty and even pain) as truly external, which is outside magical control. To control what is outside, one has to *do* things, not simply to think or to wish, and *doing things takes time.* Playing is doing" (1971, p. 47).

Winnicott does not have a simple definition of play, which he describes in many ways, but in most of his writings his description of play includes transitional phenomena or a potential space. From my point of view, this is very important when we look at play in psychotherapy in general. Winnicott also emphasizes this in his well-known quotation:

> "Psychotherapy takes place in the overlap of two areas of playing, that of the patient and that of the therapist. Psychotherapy has to do with two people playing together. The corollary of this is that where playing is not possible, then the work done by the therapist is directed towards bringing the patient from a state of not being able to play into a state of being able to play" (1971, p. 44).

Empirical research and imaginative play

In line with Winnicott's view, academic research also shows play to be important for child development. Russ (2004) presents an overview in her book. She uses the expression "pretend play" and defines it thus:

> "Pretend play involves pretending, the use of fantasy and make-believe, and the use of symbolism" (2004, p. 2).

This definition can also cover the expression "imaginative play", which is the term used for the rest of this paper.

Russ concludes that imaginative play relates to, or facilitates:

1. Problem solving that requires insight ability.
2. Flexibility in problem solving.
3. Divergent thinking ability.
4. The ability to think of alternative coping strategies when dealing with daily problems and the ability to cope.
5. The experiencing of positive emotion.
6. The ability to think about and express both positive and negative affect themes in other situations.
7. The ability to understand the emotions of others and to take the perspective of another.
8. Some aspects of general adjustment.

It is an open question that the capability for imaginative play is just related to most of these abilities or if there is a causal relationship between them. Theoretically, we can hypothesize that imaginative play can enhance capacity on all eight points.

The adult who can play with reality, accept the as-if quality of the therapeutic relationship and use the therapeutic room as both real and as a kind of "play-ground", probably has the same possibility of enhancing several of the above-mentioned abilities. However, to use the therapeutic space in this way, the patient must to some degree have a mature personality structure. Patients in group analysis very often are not well integrated in their personality structure and, accordingly, it takes time for the group to reach a level of communication where play can enter as an agent for change. In my experience, it is important to be aware that there is a certain kind of play that is essential for the development of analytic groups and their participants. Therein lays the potential for destructive play.

Destructive play and creativity

In Winnicott's writings, play is connected to health but, play is not always healthy. Green (2005) mentions that play can be destructive, as in the Roman games and Russian roulette, and even football matches may become a justification for killings. In a discussion of Winnicott's theories of play, Green writes:

> "During these last few years, we have witnessed many examples of perverted playing, of dirty playing. Such play is not based on an interchange, but on the will to dominate; it is a way of imposing one's will, and the will to submit. It is a kind of play that is impregnated with destructiveness. I think that Winnicott could not accept that destructiveness could also be transformed into a sort of play that brought not only a kind of enjoyment, but also a way of feeding one's omnipotence" (2005, p. 12).

Perhaps the above examples describe games rather than play in the way Winnicott describes it. In games, there are general rules and time limits, and there is a goal; you can be a winner or a loser in the game. Games proceed more by external, fixed rules than imaginative play. Games depend more on cognitive processes and conscious thinking. In play, there is no clear purpose or goal; play is voluntary and does not have a time limit which is planned beforehand. There are differences between games and children's play in general, but some kinds of children's play are connected more to games and some to imaginative play. Role-play includes both rules of the game and imaginative play. In psychotherapy with adults, the border between game and play is more blurred. Green does not give concrete examples of 'dirty' playing, but his description of destructive play is useful nonetheless.

Green (2005) sees treacherous, cruel and destructive play not only as a form of non-playing, but also as a counterpart to playing; negative playing. He compares it to a negative therapeutic reaction, where domination and submission come into play. Green's point is that the specificity of play in both forms, changes reality into something else, something that transforms what is unbearable in reality, be it internal or external.

A clinical example may illustrate this. The example is from one of my groups, an analytic group which has been running for three years. There are seven members in the group, four men and three women.

> It has for some time been obvious that Mr M and Ms F are attracted to each other. At one session, Mr M says openly that he feels very attracted to Ms F, and she responds that she also feels attracted to him. The two of them talk more about their mutual attraction and say it is a pity they are in the group together, so they cannot be lovers in reality. Ms F says that in a way she is relieved, because she knows about Mr M's way of living, so being lovers in reality would probably rapidly become a catastrophe, at least for her. The rest of the group is quiet until I ask what reactions they might have. There are different reactions, some are jealous; some say it is good that they bring it up openly. I take the opportunity to work therapeutically with Mr M's and Ms F's attraction to each other and with the obvious connection to their real life problems. I suggest that they work with the challenge in the group.
>
> **But** four weeks later, Ms F phones me before the session and tells me that Mr M and she have been meeting for some weeks and have had sex together. At first I am shocked, later on I become angry and in doubt as to what to do. I invite her and Mr M to come to the group and talk about what to do in the next session, for instance, whether they can continue in the group.
>
> Both are present for the next group meeting and Mr M tells the group how he put a message with his phone number on Ms F's car. Ms F recounts that she also had wanted to make contact with Mr M. They have been together several times but have agreed to stop seeing each other and hope to be able to continue in therapy. Both of them recognize that therapy will be destroyed if they continue the relationship outside the group. Ms F feels guilty and is very afraid of being rejected by the group. Mr M does not feel guilty and defends himself saying that, if I exclude him from the group, it will simply be a pity. He can manage on his own.

By coming back to the group and talking about their acting-out, Mr M and Ms F were asking for help to stop the destructive relationship.

Mr M and Ms F did continue in the group and, although this was quite difficult for the group to contain, it survived as a therapeutically powerful group. Both Mr M and Ms F managed partly to change their destructive patterns

By having sex, Mr M and Ms F destroyed their possibility of playing freely in fantasy with their relationship. The real relationship restricted the possible fantasized images of their relationship. If they had kept playing, verbally and emotionally in the group with their desires, they would have been able to a much greater degree, to have become conscious of the anxiety and the defensive nature of their destructive patterns. Some group therapists would probably have rejected the two participants for breaking the boundaries in this way. I chose to let them stay in the group. Although I was in doubt, I thought that if the group and I could contain the feelings and reactions which were acted out by Mr M and Ms F, there would be a great potential for change, both for these two participants and for the rest of the group.

Several interpretations of what happened are possible. It is obvious that the couple's behaviour could be understood as an oedipal conflict, a rebellion against the group and the group conductor's authority. They acted on their mutual attraction and desires and enjoyed the physical satisfaction of their sexual love relationship. However, I think it is important to be open to other interpretations. The two participants were resistant to accepting the boundaries of the group and to fully becoming members of the community. However, in a way, both of them were also asking for something to be contained. Their acting out could destroy their therapy but at the same time it may be understood as a communication about something difficult to manage that had to be contained and talked about in the group. Thus play was not absent, although it was destructive play, as described by Green (2005). Accordingly, it contained a wish through play to transform something unbearable into something else.

A hypothesis could be that Mr M was afraid of being engulfed by the group, experiencing the group as a Mother, going on to utilise a well known defence mechanism: he challenged authority, thus demonstrating his autonomy, and went for a new intimate relationship with a woman. Ms F's fear was that it would be impossible for her, at one and the same time, to be part of the women's subgroup and to be herself, i.e., different from the others. These hypotheses build on Nielsen and Rudberg´s understanding of women's and men's different archaic defence mechanisms (1994). These defence mechanisms can especially be activated in a group with both female and male participants.

In creative play, it is the process that is important. As pointed out earlier, this is different from a game where the outcome is important (Richards, 2005). In the group, games can be connected to rivalry, whereas creative play is more connected to working together. Both rivalry and working together are important group experiences. When Mr M and Ms F provoked the group, for a while it also was a game. Both the group members and I had fantasies about their still being together, or kissing in the corridor. On one hand, it was possible to make a fruitful analysis of what had happened, but on the other there was a continuing feeling of being used in a kind of game. This game did not come to an end until some of the other participants disclosed their fantasies that Mr M and Ms F still had a sexual relationship, and there was open discussion of this. It became more obvious that several of the other participants were jealous and angry, and this activated issues about dominance and submission. Both Mr M and Ms F were re-enacting old patterns. Taking Mr M's history into consideration, the repetition compulsion was obvious to see. For me as a therapist, it was difficult both to be part of this repetition compulsion and still to be open to the possibility of new opportunities emerging. How could I be creative and playful when the power struggle between Mr M and myself could break out at any moment? Mr M had a dominating role in the group and so the power struggle was a question for the whole group. The other participants were mostly passive witnesses to this struggle. The survival of the group as a powerful therapeutic place was also part of the struggle. In the counter transference, I felt caught between the roles of a punishing father and a weak, neglecting mother. In time, it became possible for me to say in the group that I thought that Mr M and I had been having a power struggle and that he had been re-enacting his story. Mr M could almost accept this interpretation, although several times before in the group he had rejected this kind of interpretation.

I have focused on Mr M in this vignette because of the difficult therapeutic challenge he presented to me and also because of the obvious power struggle between him, me, and the group. But was this play? From one perspective the course of events can be understood as repetition compulsion, transference and countertransference reactions, and it may be thought that it was the interpretation of these reactions that made the change in Mr M and the group. In my view, the process foregoing my interpretation was play in which the boundaries of the group were challenged, and in which both the group and I participated in the re-enactment of both Mr M's and Ms F's story. There was both a re-enactment of a struggle and a challenge of what could be allowed here and now in the group. There was a playing part in the challenge of the group. There was something going on in a secret way but at the same time all of us knew. In the process there were therapeutic interchanges about the themes, the boundaries of the group and the difference between acting out and exploring in fantasy. The whole group process took place against a background of destructive feelings. Would the "play" collapse and would Mr M then leave the group in anger or, would I throw him out? I think it was my willingness to take part in this "play" that, over time, prepared Mr M for the interpretation and made it possible for him to accept it. He could then start to see how a part of the process was a repetition of the power struggle he had had with his father.

Transference and countertransference reactions were intertwined with process in this example. Understanding what is going on in this perspective is central in group analysis and I, as a therapist, kept this understanding in mind. When I also kept the understanding of the potentially destructive play in mind, it gave new possibilities. In play there is an interchange to which both parts contribute, and through the process of playing, new and unexpected things can happen. But play can also suddenly break down, come to an end unexpectedly. Play is a serious matter.

Mentalisation, psychic equivalence and pretend mode

According to Fonagy and Target (2000), children's development of a normal awareness of the relationship between internal and external reality is not a universal, but a developmental achievement. It is a consequence of the integration of two different mental states: psychic equivalence and the pretend mode (see below). As a result of the successful integration of these mental states, the child develops the capacity of mentalisation, the capacity to assume the existence of thoughts and feelings in oneself and in others, and to recognise these as connected to, but not identical with, outer reality. It is the basis of the ability for reflection.

The small child playing is in the pretend mode. This play is dissociated from reality. "It is just play", claims the child if it becomes too real. In the pretend mode, the child experiences feelings and ideas as totally symbolic, having no implications for the real world.

In psychic equivalence, there is an exact correspondence between internal state and external reality: how it seems is how it is. For example, if a child has touched a sponge made to look like a stone, the child will say that it *looks* like a sponge, because it is a sponge although in reality it looks like a stone. At this stage of development, the child has a so-called teleological understanding of the world. This means that the child understands the actions of others as intentional and with a purpose. But when the child is still functioning at a teleological level, the effect on the child of the other's actions is identical with the other's intentions. For example, if the father makes the child sad, the child thinks it was the father's intention to make him sad.

In healthy development, children integrate these two states of mental activity around the age of five. The "good enough" parents play with their children but also play with reality and make a firm distinction between the pretend mode and reality. As a consequence of experience and maturation, the child eventually understands the difference between the intentions of others and the effect of their actions. In normal development, the child can find itself in the eyes of the mother and the father and at the same time it can find something different. This difference is the foundation for the child to make a representation of the world and its objects. But if the parents are not able to contain the child's mental experience and think about it, the child's development can go wrong. Trauma has been shown to play a significant role in the genesis of borderline states (Johnson et al., 1999). Fonagy and Target (2000) argue that severely traumatised or abused children show evidence of this in one or more of the following ways:

1. A persistence of a psychic equivalence mode of experiencing internal reality.

2. A propensity to continue to shift into the pretend mode through dissociation. Being in the pretend mode is then not connected to reality. For example, when the patient talks about horrible experiences from his/her story in an unaffected way, it is like telling another person's story.
3. A partial inability to reflect on one's own mental states and those of one's objects.

These ways of thinking can persist into adulthood and play an important role in borderline phenomena.

These important concepts, the mode of psychic equivalence and the pretend mode, are very useful for managing the meeting between borderline patients in the group. They also help to differentiate between being in the pretend mode, where the playing is dissociated too much from reality, and being part of imaginative play, which also can be a playing with reality. I will give an example:

Ms D is 34 years old when she starts in the group. She has a borderline personality disorder and has never been able to complete any education, although she has tried many times and clearly is intelligent. She has been in the group from the start. Ms D and Ms F, mentioned earlier, have a difficult relationship in the group. The group had been running for 2½ years when this session occurred.

> Ms D tells a dream about a big woman comforting her in such a way that she can hardly breathe. It leads to her telling, in a more authentic way than previously, of her personal history. Ms F asks her some questions and Ms D shifts to her usual tense way of being in the group. I convey my observation to Ms D. She says that Ms F is just like her mother. She asks her questions in a harsh way and looks at her as if she is stupid. It is very difficult for Ms D **not** to see Ms F as a representation of her mother. She reacts by feeling as if she was a child and Ms F then is her mother. The effect of Ms F's action is, for Ms D, the same as her intention.
>
> Ms F takes it as a personal attack and says angrily to Ms D: "I just want to help you."
>
> I intervene, pointing out the re-enactment of Ms D's dream here and now in the group. Ms D calms down. Ms F tries not to react, but it is very difficult for her. Some of the group members seem to understand how Ms D re-enacts her story but one of the men is more occupied with

supporting Ms F. He says that it was unfair how Ms D reacted and that
I, the therapist, took Ms D's side.

Ms F has been quiet for some time but just half a minute before the
session ends she shouts: "I am so mad that you are always so paranoid
Ms D. You are just like my sister!"

Both Ms D and Ms F re-enact their story and go into the mode of psychic equivalence where there is no difference between inner and outer reality. It was as if both of them played a role from their own history, which at the same time was a role in the other's history. But the re-enactment and the turning up of the past in the present, is not the full story. The lived reactions here and now in the group between Ms F and Ms D became a part both of their relationship, and the history of the group. This play had an effect on the whole group. Could the group be a safe place? Will Ms D and Ms F start fighting again? Over the next month it was possible to work with these reactions and also to look at how I, as the group conductor, became part of the double triangle related to the history of both Ms F and Ms D. But now and again, arguing and verbal in-fighting broke out and both Ms F and Ms D went into the mode of psychic equivalence. At other times we could look at the re-enactment and see the as-if quality in their relationship, but for a long time it was like small children's pretend play; it was separated from reality, and they easily shifted to acting in the mode of psychic equivalence.

Ms D's dream was both informative and transformative (Friedman, 2002, 2007). In a condensed way it expressed one of her dilemmas: to be comforted in an intimate relationship means also to suffocate. In the transformative aspect of the dream, Ms D asked for help to stop the "comforting" woman both inside and outside. Some of the group members responded to her request to develop the capacity to be in a close relationship without feeling suffocated. Others played the role of the "comforting" woman, which Ms D immediately experienced as suffocating her. The dream was inter-personally re-created in the group.

Different levels of communication

Foulkes (1990), the founder of group analysis, described the different levels of communication in a group. Foulkes differentiates between a level with the group as forum, a level representing whole-objects, the family, a level with part-objects, a body level and an archaic level connecting to Jung's concept of the collective unconscious. One level of communication will be in the foreground and the others in the background. During a session, the level in the foreground can shift few or many times. I will focus on the archaic or primordial level.

One way to realise that the group is communicating at the archaic or primordial level is to notice that the language and the images and metaphors are more archaic. Just as poetry is not the thing said but the way of saying it, archaic language is a way of weighting words with the cadence of earlier destinies. Metaphors and images are rooted in natural phenomena. They can turn up in glimpses or can be major changes in the discourse of the group session and may be connected to one member and his or her story. First an example of such a moment:

> In the group of women recovering from anorexia, Ms Q tells about a period when she ate a lot of chocolate. She calls it the "time of choco-late". Now she is eating ice cream. Then suddenly she says, maybe it is the Ice Age! This changed the communication in the group. It became more intense and at the same time more playful. We talked about how the Ice Age had formed our country. The Ice Age had a very fundamental importance for how we lived. Metaphorically, we could talk about both inner and outer reality at the same time.

There was a change in communication in several ways. The metaphor "Ice Age" started the communication at the primordial level; at this point in the group discussion this level came into the foreground. The playing aspect emerged with the double meaning that we talked about, both Ms Q's "relation" to chocolate and ice cream and the more general, old and basic conditions for human beings.

With the primordial level in the foreground, it is difficult to describe the form of communication. It cannot be done in a concrete and precise way. Perhaps it can only be done in images or metaphorically. Changing to this level of communication is like going through the gate to the Kingdom of Narnia (Lewis, 2002). In Narnia, time is different. A day in Narnia is only a minute in normal reality. If once a King or Queen in Narnia, you will always be a King or Queen in Narnia. But when you have changed in the Kingdom of Narnia, when you have fulfilled your quest in this other reality, you will also change in normal reality. This is a way to describe what happens when psychotherapy enters the primordial level in play and the participants begin to use dream images or mutative metaphors. In psychotherapy, it is experienced as being in another state of mind, maybe only for a short time in reality, although it can feel like a long time when it happens.

Following Ms D in her ongoing journey through the therapeutic process in the group may take us further into this other reality.

It is important to clarify some of the context for the session described as at that time, I was preoccupied with the integration of the Aeolian mode of psychotherapy in my way of conducting the group. I will provide a short summary of the Aeolian mode, as described by Cox & Theilgaard (1987). The Aeolian Mode is more a playing attitude of the therapist, than it is a technique. The name comes from the Aeolian harp: a wind harp which is so loosely tuned that its strings can catch the slightest breeze and turn it into music. The harp plays the music of nature. The Aeolian mode has as its aim, to bring about change in psychotherapy in a way which is described briefly in the following quotation from Gaston Bachelard:

> "But the image has touched the depths before it stirs the surface" (quoted in Cox & Theilgaard, 1987, p. xiii).

The therapist working in the Aeolian Mode is open to images and metaphors which can create images that touch the depths before they stir the surface. The therapist is in a creative process, but he is not inventing the images, he perceives them. In the Aeolian Mode there is a search for what Bateson (1979) calls, "the pattern which connects." It is a search in which both the patient and the therapist participate, although they approach the scene from different starting points. Furthermore, there is an inescapable aspect of threshold-crossing in which they are both engaged. For the patient, this involves the threshold between the unconscious and the conscious, which may be crossed by words or images.

The therapist's threshold is a different one, and it is a double threshold. It is, in part, that of discerning "the pattern which connects" and is also in part, that of being present with his patient, through empathy and transference, as the threshold of insight is crossed.

The Aeolian Mode consists of the synergism between three dynamic components:

- *Poiesis*: a process by which something is called into existence which was not there before.
- *Aesthetic imperative*: the therapist's experience of a sense of "fit" and coherence, linked to an imperative urge to respond to a patient in a particular way.
- *Points of urgency*: a moment of incipient dynamic instability, in which the endopsychic patterning is such that the patient is optimally receptive to the therapist's initiative.

Clinical example:

> Ms D starts recounting that she has been offered a new position at her workplace. A position she would like to take. She had for a long time been feeling good, but now she feels very depressed. She tells about a dream: she stole something not very valuable, and for this she was sentenced to 30 years in jail. She is carrying her son, but he is only two years old, so this must have happened a long time ago. Later in the dream she met some girlfriends from primary school.
>
> Listening to her dream, I think at once of Ms D's story, of the triangle between her and her parents, with her being in or out of the relationship. I also think of how she was told that it was her making noise which caused her father's epileptic seizures. As a child she believed he could die from his epileptic seizures. I thought of her dream as describing a life-sentence: "I am not allowed to feel good and use my resources, then my father and mother will die. I am going to be a victim all my life." The sentence is not entirely meaningful, but very strong in me. There are some discussions in the group about Ms D's dream, but being sent to jail makes no sense. I ask myself whether I should share my thoughts. It is the last session before the summer break. Would it affect Ms D too much?
>
> But then she asks me directly, "Do you think I have depression and need anti-depressant drugs?"

Then I feel that I have to share my thoughts and I say, "I think your dream tells us that you are captured in a prison. You are sentenced to 30 years in prison for a minor criminal act. It is not clear who is punishing you. I do not think you have depression for which you need anti-depressant drugs, but you have a pattern of attacking yourself every time you are developing and starting to use more of your resources. It is a kind of masochistic pattern and you become a victim. This pattern is created by your history."

Ms D responds by saying, "You say, I am not allowed to feel good. Then everything will go wrong?"

It was nearly the end of the session, so only a short time was left for further discussion but, after the summer break, Ms D had thought about this pattern and the image of being sentenced to prison for 30 years for only a minor criminal act. She was much more aware of how she keeps making herself a victim.

The images of the prison and the unfair sentence were called into existence by her dream and it was connected to a life-sentence which turned up in me. Ms D was at a point of urgency where she was optimally receptive. A connecting pattern was made apparent and it was further developed in the time after the session, becoming a turning point for Ms D. Something new was called into existence.

But the image of the prison and the unfair sentence also resonated in the group and in me. The image of an unfair sentence for something which had happened a long time ago resonated on a primordial level. The word primordial has different meanings: original, oldest, fundamental and universal. The dream image created the possibility of seeing a fundamental (archaic) and penetrating pattern in Ms D. In the group, it brought the image of the punishing but hidden authority, The Law, into consciousness. It was difficult for the group to translate the image of the prison, but it made a confusing impact.

During the following months, Ms D returned to the experience and used the image of the prison and connected it to her story. Sometimes we played with the image. Could she escape? How would that be? Connected to the images was the recreation of some of the different atmospheres present in the group when the images came up in the first place. It was like opening the gate to Narnia. By playing with the important dream in this way, Ms D developed in several ways. Specifically, her capacity to think on her own of alternative, coping strategies in her daily life was developed. But it also became easier for her to take another person's perspective without losing her own, or herself. The playing was now imaginative; it was a play in fantasy which was no longer dissociated from reality, as I described previously with the example of the interchange between Ms D and Ms F. Ms D could now take part in joint play and still have a double consciousness. It influenced her life and reality in two of the ways that Russ (2004) describes as possible positive outcomes of imaginative play: the ability to think of alternative coping strategies when dealing with daily problems, the ability to cope, the ability to understand the emotions of others and to take the perspective of another.

Looking back, we could see this as an important turning point in her journey towards separating from her self-defeating pattern and in the end, separating from the group and being able to live a life on her own.

It also had an effect on the group, but in telling this story about Ms D, I have put her in the foreground and the group in the background. Some group members easily followed the process: they took part in the play and imaginative work, while others found it difficult to understand and to play along.

At her last session, Ms D brought one of her son's creations. He had made it as a container for his Game Boy games, but it looked like a small prison. For Ms D, this represented her quest for freedom. Now she had the key herself to the door of the prison. So the prison could also be a safe place in which to seek protection when necessary.

Play is mostly understood as play with fantasy and images in a joint interchange which affects the participants. It is an example of "the overlap of two areas of playing", although in the group it will be more than two. Following the development of the group I have drawn examples from, it becomes obvious that it takes time and a lot of therapeutic work to reach this level of communication. The group has to be quite mature to be able to play in this way. However, on its way to reaching maturity, my group did in fact play, although that was another kind of play. It was potentially destructive play; pretend-play dissociated from reality. When the group and the therapist contain and take part in this kind of play, the group and the individual members may develop the capacity for joint imaginative play with a double consciousness. This play has the potential to change both the group and its participants, and it gives better opportunities for using the group creatively. This kind of play is often connected to a change in the level of the group's communication towards primordial communication, in which archaic images and metaphors come to life. The archaic images and metaphors will, at the same time, be connected both to the history of one or more of the members in the group and to the common cultural history.

The joint imaginative play has a time and a place. The play does not have a particular purpose, you just play. At the primordial level of communication, in a way it is the same: the dialogue does not have a specific purpose or goal, the dialogue is just on-going. The images and the metaphors which come into existence can both connect and contain differences at the same time. The interchanges at this level, take place in a more analogical than a digital way.

Conclusion

Play is an essential part of every human's life. From the beginning of life we start to play. We start in interaction; our play is embodied and concrete and only later involves pretending. This is as adults understand it. From the perspective of the baby it is being, or being in the world, or maybe being the world. Children interact and play when their life-essential needs are fulfilled. The capacity for imaginative play builds on the early interaction between the baby and its caregiver. In child psychiatry, we often see children who have an apparently rich fantasy and can play on their own, but they lack the capacity to play in a reciprocal way. Only when play is imaginative **and** reciprocal can it change reality. Children can play alone and through the play they can handle emotional reactions raised by their reality. In the same way, adults can reflect when alone. When the child *plays in the presence* of a therapist, something else happens. Then the play is both play and has a communicative aspect. In group analysis, for adults, it corresponds to having witnesses when telling your story. When the play becomes part of an interaction or even reciprocal, the capacity for change is much greater. If you have the courage to go into this playful interaction, almost certainly something new is called into existence. At least for a moment, change has happened. Winnicott says: "the significant moment is that at which *the child surprises himself or herself"* (1971, p. 59). The same is true in both group psychotherapy and individual psychotherapy with adults.

When play has the power to change, it is a reciprocal interaction where something new is created, and it is at the borderline between pretending and reality. All the participants know it is play, but it should not be said aloud. Often the play is very serious but every participant is allowed to say, "Stop, we are only playing". If everybody plays according to the rules, the play will stop.

In the group, there is a constant change of what is in the foreground and the background: here and now, or reality outside the group, one member, or the whole group. Playing makes a double meaning possible; talking about two perspectives at the same time. In this way, playing with reality becomes part of the imaginative play, here and now. But this will only work for the participant who has the capacity to mentalize or reflect. Members who have difficulties with the integration of the mode of psychic equivalence and the pretend mode, will have difficulties using playing in the group in this way. Their capacity for imaginative play has to be developed during the therapeutic process.

Play and dream are closely connected. Both in dreaming and in playing the psyche creates images which can mean several things at the same time. Sometimes the group plays with a dream told by one of the participants. But if playing with the dream in the group becomes a game about coming up with the most spectacular images or associations to the dream, then the dream-teller can be offended or alienated. On the other hand, playing with dream-images which in some way have been connected to the conscious life can be a creative and changing process for both the group and the dream-teller. Dream-telling in the group can be seen as both a quest for having something unbearable contained, and a wish for "pushing" the relation in a certain direction (Friedman, 2007). In both of the dreams Ms D re-told in the group, there are power issues. There is someone who is "opposed to play", either a law or a big woman suffocating her when she needs containing. The father could die if she played joyfully and freely as a child. This struggle between the drive for playing and punishment, which Ms. D shows so clearly, has been one of the reasons for choosing her to exemplify how play has the power to effect change in group analysis. At the same time, it is a story about strong forces opposed to playfulness and personal change. Play can be experienced as dangerous, strange or even forbidden, but it certainly has the power to create change in psychotherapy.

A commentary on Peter Ramsing's article 'Has play the power to change group and patients in group analysis?'

Jacinta Kennedy

Introduction

Peter Ramsing, in his article "Has Play the Power to Change Group and Patients in Group Analysis?", has made a powerful argument for adult play in the group as being a useful developmental or reconstructive process, and provided several examples of how play and metaphor in the group, may lead to changes in perception and experiencing within the group setting. Therefore, it would seem important that the group analyst encourage play in the healthy group. A failure to play for the individual, shows inhibition and disturbance in thinking in relation to others, according to Melanie Klein (1929), and this may also apply to the group.

The article gives rise to many questions about the therapeutic possibilities of play in group analysis and in doing so, opens up several issues about the boundaries of play. There is positive play where the adult can accept the as-if quality of the therapeutic space as real, and as a playground, according to Peter, and also negative play, described by Green (2005) which is imbued with destructiveness and domination, but which is also capable of changing reality into something else. However, can the clinician easily distinguish between the two in the group setting? As Winnicott (1971) noted, play is "inherently exciting and precarious". What is tolerable for one group member may lead to excessive anxiety and fear of loss of control for another, depending on group members' history and psychopathology.

Group boundaries and playing

It seems that for playing to occur, the conductor themselves must have some capacity for playing and be free from excessive anxiety, such that it is possible to attune and respond to the individual or group gesture, perhaps in a "marked" or non-verbally expressive way, described by Stern (1985) as how the sensitive mother responds to the infant. However, the conductor must also, through their attitude and engagement in the dynamic administration of the group, reflect the paternal function representing order, structure and boundaries.

Peter has illustrated an accommodating, containing and playful response, principally aimed at the developmental meaning for the two individuals engaged in the acting out, which appeared intuitive, empathic and clinically containing. However, this does not address how the paternal function must also be invoked in the group. Could it be that the paternal "No", was not sufficiently present or not sufficiently taken up in the group, when the two members declared their attraction initially? Taking a group perspective on the acting out of the "couple", it might also be seen as a manifestation of the borderline functioning of the group as a whole, with an attack on the containing mother or matrix.

Viewing acting out as negative play may therefore leave the group and the conductor in a vulnerable position, and there will be times when an empathic, developmentally based response is not enough. The conductor may need to meet the member's or group's gesture with more than thought or reverie. Hook (1999) speaks about the need for the conductor to meet action with thought-and-action in the case of high risk. She suggests that when, for example, suicide is threatened, the conductor's containment may well include action, such as providing individual sessions, consultation with other professionals, etc.

Perhaps it is important to separate destructive fantasies from destructive acts and limit what could be described as negative play to fantasy? Nitsun's (1996) concept of the anti-group as a "broad term for describing the destructive aspect of groups that threatens the integrity of the group and its therapeutic development" is of relevance here. The anti-group has the potential to generate a constructive process in an ongoing cycle of creation and negation in a dialectical process (Nitsun, 1999). Thus, when destructive fantasies are spoken of in the group, there comes the potential for change. However, when destructive fantasies are acted out, it is much more difficult for the group and the conductor to survive. In Peter's example, both the conductor and the group survived, but this is not always the case as destructive acting out in the clinical situation may also lead to losses of group members or the collapse of the group. This is particularly the case when there is a predominance of borderline functioning in the group, when it is imperative that boundaries are firmly held.

Surviving negative play/destructive fantasies and acts

Destructive fantasies and destructive behaviour may take some time for the conductor to discern, or may appear suddenly or violently in the group. This constitutes a formidable clinical challenge, when the main task of the conductor is to survive him/herself and also work towards the survival of the group. Perhaps Knauss's (1999) reflections on the preconditions for survival point to a more complex requirement for the conductor:

1. A conscious access to our own destructive fantasies in the countertransference.
2. An accepting attitude towards destructive fantasies.
3. An understanding of the developmental meaning of the fantasies.
4. Creating an environment for ourselves and for the patient so that we have a better chance of surviving.

Nitsun (1996) has carefully delineated the determinants of the Anti-Group and among other factors, noted the importance of projective identification and envy in the emergence of the anti-group. However, if the anti-group becomes represented as play, even negative play, we may lose sight of the fact that it is also a flight from inner reality to outward reality, as Resnik (1999) points out. The acting out requires not just containing but analysis of transference-countertransference, processing and returning that which has been projected by interpretation of unconscious group dynamics. These must be addressed and worked through, such that reflective space can be restored, the boundaries held and the anxieties of the group returned to tolerable levels. A group conductor therefore, has the difficult job of not being either in too playing nor too working a mode, but perhaps has to have flexibility in being able to respond to the group gesture from both perspectives.

A final point in terms of considering negative play or the emergence of the anti-group is what role the conductor him/herself has consciously or unconsciously played in the emergence of destructive fantasies or acts. This points to the need for careful reflection and supervision on behalf of the group analyst, especially when there is severe disturbance in the group.

Gender-specific defences and identity development

A further issue which might be explored is the use of a gender-specific model of development to interpret defence mechanisms in the group. This may be a limited model for an adult group: a gendered, fixed identity as a theoretical basis which may, as Burman (2005) notes, lead to the making of prescriptive assumptions about what is normal or abnormal. This binary view of gender identity may not reflect the diversity of identities and expressions of sexuality the group analyst meets within the adult group. Burman (2005) argues that a feminist perspective has much to offer group analysis with its emphasis on plurality of gender and sexuality, the notions of gender and sexuality being performative, rather than an expression of some inner, stable identity and intersecting whereby gender intersects with, rather than providing the foundations for, sexuality. Perhaps this latter view would be more enabling of discourse in the group, allowing the group to explore their fantasized and real experiences of gender and sexuality, in fact, allowing members to "play" with sexuality within the group.

Play in group analysis

In the move from concrete reality to the as-if mode, there is something inherently playful in all forms of analysis. Nevertheless, in group analysis, the potential for play may be even greater due to the nature of the free-floating discussion and how members' narratives interweave in the matrix. Stacey (2005) describes conversational processes where there is a transformational potential, "... liveliness, fluidity and energy, but also a feeling of grasping at meaning and coherence ...". This is very close to the felt experience of a well communicating analytic group and perhaps is useful in helping us to recognise that our ordinary work in group analysis is playful. Group analytic creativity does not rely on occasions where metaphorical communication arises, yet may be greatly deepened and universalised by this phenomenon.

CHAPTER THREE

The power of hate in therapy

Mette Kjær Barfort

Therapists working with clients who suffer from personality disorders, especially those who are severely narcissistic, are inevitably exposed to intense emotions of hate and hateful fantasies. In my own clinical practice, I find it very challenging at times to deal with the powerful projections from this group of clients whose inner world and relationships are dominated by hate. Hateful clients have very little faith, sometimes no faith at all, in the existence of goodness in themselves and in others, and as a defensive reaction, they tend to attack and destroy their therapists' empathy and interventions simply because they are experienced as threatening to their psychic existence. When exposed to these hateful attacks, strong countertransference feelings are evoked in the therapist, who may be experiencing the whole spectrum of emotions from anger and hate to guilt, despair and depression.

The strong emotion of hate can be enacted violently and overtly but is frequently transmitted through primitive forms of powerful projective identifications. This hateful non-verbal communication from the client is not always easy to register and understand for the therapist. They may feel overwhelmed and unable to maintain their own sense of analytic space and be unable to function as a container of the client's hateful emotions. My focus in this paper is to look into what kind of powerful forces are at stake in therapy when the client is full of hate, and the therapist is filled with countertransference feelings while at the same time, struggling to maintain a neutral, playful and exploratory approach.

I will illustrate the power of hate in the therapeutic relationship with a case from my own practice:

> C is a man with a severely narcissistic personality disorder who has made several attempts at suicide. He has very little contact with other people, due to persecutory fantasies and anxiety. He grew up with a mentally ill father, whom he was afraid of, and a mother whose ability to show empathy and to take care of C was limited. He was very jealous of his sisters, who in his opinion, the parents preferred to him. The relationship with his mother was characterized by her controlling, and at times, sadistic behaviour. C sees himself as a victim and especially blames his mother that he is not able to have a normal life. He imagines that if he could get his mother's unconditional love, all his troubles would disappear, without his taking any responsibility at all. C seems unconsciously to refuse to become strong and more independent as this would mean letting his mother off the hook and not be punished for the damage she has done to him.
>
> In relationships with others, C sees himself as a victim of other peoples' self-interests, dislike and hate towards him. He appears at first sight shy, anxious and suffering. The therapist, however, soon experiences that C has another, dissociated part of his personality, full of envy and hate. He is extremely envious of other peoples' lives and seems to be bound by an unconscious urge to make the other suffer and feel the severe pain which he himself feels. He consciously and unconsciously makes efforts to provoke the therapist into acting in a certain role from his inner scenario, thereby fulfilling his fearful expectations while attempting to control her, basically in order to limit her dangerousness.
>
> By means of projective identification, C's internal world of victim and victimizer, of slave and tyrant, is enacted in such a way that the therapist is assigned the role of the victim or slave, and he the role of the victimizer or sadistic tyrant.
>
> C enters therapy expecting the therapist to be a fairy godmother with a magic wand, who will be able to make him feel good, and who

literally will take responsibility for his life, without his making any effort himself. His conscious awareness of hate is mostly split-off, and the therapist is exposed to an intensely hateful projection which often takes place without words. C is suffering, and by both verbal and non-verbal communication, he lets her know that his pain gets worse, for example by arrogant, hateful dismissal of whatever good comes from her for example, when she ends sessions without giving him extra time, when she does not let him call her on the phone between sessions and so on. His masochistic appearance combined with his humiliating and contemptuous attacks puts her under strong pressure. The devaluating statements about the therapist secretly provide C with an enormous pleasure in the sessions. The therapist feels more and more invaded, anxious, hateful, guilty, passive, and disempowered, reduced to fulfilling the needs of C. She feels taken hostage by C's non-verbal suicidal threats and feels either all-bad, as the internalized, persecutory object, a person who has the power to make C kill himself, or all-good, as the internalized, idealized object, the idealized mother who fulfils all the needs of C. Momentarily, the therapist feels a bit crazy, experiencing a similar paranoid-schizoid universe as C.

She is responding to a projective identification from C. Moreover, she is also reacting to her own anxiety in the face of a situation where she feels that she has very little control, and where she feels like a de-skilled therapist because of her guilt over her feelings of hate. At times she also feels lonely, the guilt preventing her from sharing her experience of C with other therapists.

Hate

The origin of hate is a complex topic and raises the discussion whether hate is primarily related to a death instinct, to what extent hate is genetically determined (Klein, 1957; Kernberg, 1992, 2004) or, to what extent primarily an emotional reaction to extreme frustration (Winnicott, 1947, 1971). Similar to Winnicott, I view hate as an emotional reaction to extremely painful experiences due to deficits in the environment, but this discussion is beyond the topic of this article.

Compared to pathological hate, ordinary hate is a more acute episodical feeling of extreme rage, bound to concrete and specific circumstances, with an urge to act spontaneously in order to eliminate the frustration and pain, or to revenge oneself. It has a transitory quality, meaning that it can be let go of when circumstances change to the better, and it is mainly ego-dystonic. In spite of its emotional intensity and power, ordinary hate can be modified and mitigated by love and goodness. Usually objects of our ordinary hate remain split off or isolated from other areas of our life, which means that hate does not corrupt all our relationships (Kernberg, 1992, 2004; Akhtar, 1999).

In hateful clients, there seems to be confusion between love and hate, with no ability to distinguish one from the other, with hate dominating over love. The problem of the client with pathological hate, where pain has been transformed into rage and chronic rage into hate, is that there is very little or nothing at all in opposition to hate that can modify or balance its strong power. Hateful clients are not able to integrate the loving and hateful representations of significant others into an ambivalently perceived whole object. Instead, they are full of malicious contempt because the good, caring self and object representations lie deeply buried in order to avoid being destroyed by the premeditated hate.

Pathological hate is more chronic, stable and characterologically anchored in the client's psyche than normal hate, and is mainly ego-syntonic (Kernberg, ibid.; Akhtar, ibid.). At the most primitive level, hate reflects the desire to destroy the object perceived as bad; at a more advanced level, where there has been a fusion between early aspects of sexual excitement and hate, the aim of hate is to induce suffering in the object. At a still more advanced level, where hate has become more circumscribed, it represents the wish to dominate and control the bad object as a precondition for the safety of the self (Clarkin et al., 1999).

Hate is rooted in past, inner object-relationships which include severe pain and a person's experience that the significant other deliberately has tried to control, attack or otherwise threaten them (Kernberg, 1992, 2004). Hate is a defence against getting into contact with the underlying longing for the love and care that the person originally felt, in relationship to the other. Balint calls hate the immortalization of the total dependence on the primary love object with the only difference that plus is changed to minus (Balint, 1968). Klein points out that hating is holding on to an inner object in an unforgiving way (Klein, 1957). Mann describes hate as Eros with poisoned arrows in a destructive form of love (Mann, 2006).

Hate has the role of *maintaining connectedness*. Mann (2006) points out that the aim of hate is not a drive towards disconnection, freedom from emotional attachment, or an attempt at living in an objectless world. On the contrary, although awful, explosive and corrosive, hate gives a passionate attachment to others. Hate does not have as its purpose to destroy the object, but to preserve and maintain it. Hate may include a wish for death, to murder oneself or the other, but in itself, it is a form of connection, although at a safer distance than love, in order to minimize helplessness and abandonment. Hate is at times the only way in which the client is able to be in a relationship with the other. Only through hate can he tie the other in a passionate involvement with him. Only then he can feel alive and connected (Bollas, 1987; Gabbard, 1996).

> *Another client of mine, S, has been in therapy for 6 years working with paranoid and hateful fantasies in the transference situation. She has been extremely envious and hateful towards the therapist, and has had very little faith in goodness in herself and in others. Gradually this has changed through therapy and at the present moment she has gained more confidence in herself and in others, and can talk about her hate in a symbolic way that can even be playful and exploratory. She clearly expresses her fear of stopping hating the therapist because this would mean that she would get better, would not need treatment anymore and then would lose her. As long as she continues to hate the therapist, she knows that the therapist will not see her as ready to end therapy, and so she can keep the therapeutic relationship and prevent the therapist from forgetting her.*

This is, in a way, a positive use of hate. It is an attempt to try to keep up a relationship with a significant other; to keep the relationship alive and true. It is an attempt to involve the other in a passionate form of relating, even though it is fulfilled through the cultivation of negative experiences.

Countertransference evoked by hate

Countertransference, provoked by hateful clients with severe personality disorders, frequently differs from what is experienced with clients with milder disorders or neurotic personality organisation by being far more intense, difficult to contain and not possible to verbalize directly. Countertransference can be defined as the total emotional reaction of the therapist to the client at any particular point in time in therapy (Kernberg, 2004). It is a channel of communication in which the client is trying both to evacuate and to share hateful feelings and experiences. Therefore, conceptualizing this in countertransference analysis is an essential aspect of therapy, lest the therapist be overwhelmed by the process and lose contact with the client (Rosenfeld, 1987). It is important however, to understand that countertransference is a phenomenon created by both client and therapist, meaning that both the client's projected aspects and the therapist's past conflicts are working together. Consequently, it is important to differentiate between what belongs to the client and to the therapist respectively. The therapist must thus keep focus on both an intrapsychic and an interpersonal aspect in trying to understand what is going on in the client, and contain this in themselves (Kernberg, 2000, 2004; Gabbard & Wilkinson, 1994).

The countertransference feelings that are evoked in the therapist when hate is played out have both an objective quality, meaning that any therapist would tend to react in the same way, and a subjective quality, relating to the specific object relations, the current emotional state and the personality organisation of the therapist. As therapists, we differ in the way we are comfortable with hate in ourselves and in others, from reacting aggressively and offensively to reacting more fearfully and defensively. It is a major challenge for the therapist not to act out their countertransference feelings, but to contain and explore them, and it requires personal strength and maturity on the part of the therapist.

The therapist frequently experiences negative countertransference feelings, which are not consistent with the image they have of themselves as a good and caring professional. It challenges their ability to contain antagonistic feelings of wanting both to help and punish or hurt the client without acting this out, especially when they are confused and do not understand what is going on at the moment in the session. Working with hateful clients implies a paradox, in the sense that the therapist must seek to control their countertransference, but at the same time must realize that when intense, prolonged, hateful, projective identifications dominate the therapy, some degree of acting out on the part of the therapist almost inevitably occurs. It is not easy for the therapist to face their acting out; it generates guilt, shame and anxiety, and because of this, it requires courage to openly share the mistake of acting out with other colleagues.

When the therapist is exposed to the client's intense hate, their defence against their own hate is undermined. Feeling their own hate towards the client, experiencing revengeful fantasies, a sadistic urge to ridicule or even punish the client and to get rid of the client, shakes the picture of being a caring and good helper. It is frightening that even the most hateful and murderous part of the client has a resonance in the therapist (Gabbard & Wilkinson, 1994).

The power of the primitive, hateful, projective identification can be so strong and mutually experienced, it is as if there were a struggle of power or a life and death struggle going on between client and therapist. When the therapist momentarily is filled with sadistic and revengeful fantasies, this may evoke intense anxiety and paranoid fantasies in them even though they have no rational or realistic reason. These feelings may again lead to the therapist feeling a bit crazy and ashamed of their countertransference anxiety.

Depending on what kind of personal reaction the therapist is predisposed to, guilt or shame can easily arise when they are fed up with the client. Another countertransference reaction may be to turn the hate towards oneself in an excessive, masochistic self-doubt and a feeling of being all-bad. The therapist can be intensely concerned about thinking of the client outside treatment sessions. They can deny their hate towards the client or, change it to the opposite by taking on the role as all-good and try to rescue the client and tolerate extraordinarily destructive or bad behaviour from them. The therapist can furthermore avoid feeling their hate by withdrawing emotionally, being distant, bored and indifferent towards the client, or withdrawing into aloof silence.

It evokes anxiety in the therapist when they experience the paranoid-schizoid universe of the client; a universe filled with hateful, murderous and sadistic fantasies of control and destruction, with very little possibility of being mitigated or made up for by an expectation of being met by a good and caring object. Any sign of goodness must be attacked and destroyed because of the anxiety that it evokes in the client.

When hateful projections are at their most intense, the therapist can, in the same way as the client, collapse into a paranoid-schizoid mode of experience. In this mode of symbolic thinking, the "as-if" quality disappears and the therapist can feel invaded, controlled and anxious and lose their own ability to think. This can be so strong that they begin to doubt their own opinions and statements and at times, their own sanity. The therapist can experience that the client has power over them and is keeping them in a tight grip. Gabbard (1996) points out that therapists often have to balance on the verge of despair, where they seriously begin to doubt their own ability to continue as therapists, before they can get to the most primitive transference themes in their borderline-clients. Winnicott (1947) also points out that this dark and threatening place, where both the client and the therapist are at the point of giving up, is maybe the only form of transference where the client's most destructive impulses can be analysed.

Hate and envy

Rosenfeld (1987) brings a group of clients into focus who are consciously intensely destructive and sadistic, and proud of it. He talks about the pathology of destructive narcissism, where there is an enormous idealization of the destructive parts of the self which are felt to be attractive because they make the client feel omnipotent and superior.

Any wish for loving and caring object relationships and any attempt on the part of the self to experience the need for an object and to depend on it, are devalued, attacked and destroyed *with pleasure*. The idealized destructive aspects of the self and the omnipotent wishes are not easy to recognize in what a client does and says, because the client unconsciously and secretly experiences them as protective and even benevolent. Secrecy is part of omnipotent, destructive superiority. The idealized, omnipotent, destructive aspects of the self, capture and trap the positive dependent aspects. Clients dominated by destructive narcissism give the impression that they have no interest at all in other people while in fact, on the contrary, they deeply depend on constantly attacking anything and everything which might be likely to satisfy their needs for love and dependency. "Anything which might enable the client to become aware of how completely dominated and imprisoned by his omnipotence he is, is silently criticized, belittled, devaluated and distorted" (ibid., p. 87). Getting better means that the client is attacked by the primitive sadistic superego, and also that he feels guilty because he is betraying the idealized omnipotent part of his self-image. Any good, dependent relationship with the therapist is attacked and belittled.

Although C as previously mentioned, is extremely lonely, in my view he destroys all mutual relationships of which he is not in control. He idealizes his destructive and omnipotent parts and is filled with a sense that good persons are weak and unreliable. Either he becomes extremely dependent on the therapist by believing that she is responsible for his life and thereby becomes parasitic in trying to achieve a life through her, or, he attacks and devalues her. He sincerely needs the therapist as an object whom he can try to control, punish and destroy and at the same time, fears that he will succeed in this.

The therapist gets a strong feeling of this client's inner world which is full of objects which can be split-off, idealized and all-good, but are mostly all-bad, cruel, exploring, manipulative and only focused on gaining power. The client is full of unconscious, primitive envy when he sees that the therapist is not controlled by an inner world full of violence but, on the contrary, is free to feel satisfied and creative and able to enjoy the company of other people. These are qualities he himself is not able to feel, but basically needs and is longing for. Envy of her creativity evokes an unconscious urge to destroy it by gaining control over her and making her play the role which is written in his inner object-relation scenario. When envy is exceedingly marked, paranoid traits are especially strong. Hate and envy also arise in the client when he realises that he needs the therapist, that he is not totally self-sufficient, and that he is dependent on her. Envy is easily aroused by good interpretations because they expose some weakness in the client, who experiences this as a severe narcissistic blow and feels humiliated (Klein, 1957; Rosenfeld, 1987). When the client gets better, he experiences this as a result of the therapist's superiority and high intelligence, and therefore feels belittled and threatened by his own success. Furthermore, even though the narcissistic client is longing for success, they also fear that they will induce in others the same sort of hate and envy that they feel towards the creativity and success of other people. The narcissistic client must experience that everything that is valuable in the external world is part of them, or at least is controlled by them.

The envious client is not able to feel pleasure, joy or gratefulness. This is, in fact, a major problem, because it is precisely pleasure and gratefulness which has a modifying and mollifying effect on destructive impulses and primitive envy and greed. To put it in the words of Melanie Klein, greed, envy and persecutory anxiety are intermingled and reinforce each other. Gratefulness is essential for establishing the relationship to the good object and underlies the ability to acknowledge and appreciate goodness in others and in oneself. She further points out that it is only if the analysis can get to the depths and the source of envy that one can hope the analysis can have the full effect (Klein, 1957).

Keeping the playful aspect of therapy when hate is at stake

Therapy has to do with two people playing together; it takes place in the overlap of two areas of playing, that of the patient and that of the therapist (Winnicott, 1971).

Playing is an important means of exploring the relationship between internal reality and external reality, and it is through play that we can explore and learn something essential about ourselves and others (Caper, 1999). Referring to Bion's concept of "realistic projective identification", Caper points out that the client plays with the therapist's mind by active deployment of projections and by evoking countertransference responses in them in order to see how they react and hereby to learn something important about the therapist's state of mind: "If I do this to them, what will happen?"

Another aspect of playing is to learn about one's own internal world by using the mind of the other as an instrument of measurement. The client projects aspects of their internal world into the therapist so that they may explore the nature of whatever aspect of their internal reality they are projecting into the therapist (ibid.). If the client can make the therapist feel what they feel and they see how the therapist reacts, then they can learn something about their own mind. "If the therapist gets angry, then what I am doing is something that evokes anger in others".

Playing depends on the capacity to form symbols, to preserve the distinction between the symbol itself and what is symbolized, and to keep internal and external reality separate in one's mind. "There must be a limit to what one feels is the power of one's thoughts over the mind of the object, and there must be a similar limitation on the power of the object's mind over one's own" (Caper, 1999, p. 93). When there is confusion between inner and outer reality and when symbolic thinking breaks down, the client is unable to play with the world in an experimental way, thereby unable to explore and learn about his own projections and the mind of the therapist.

When the hateful projections are at their most intense, this frequently causes a breakdown in symbolic thinking, which makes it impossible to maintain a playful approach in therapy. When playing is not possible in therapy, the work done by the therapist must be directed towards bringing the patient from a state of not being able to play into a state of being able to play (Winnicott, 1971). But how does the therapist do that?

Working with hate in therapy

Winnicott points out that some clients actively seek our hate and in fantasy need to destroy the therapist while at the same time, needing the therapist to *survive* their annihilatory hate. This will help them to get a sense of the limits of their destructive fantasies and also help them to realize that no matter how hateful or murderous their wishes are, the therapist can still survive. Thereby, the clients can begin to see the therapist as a real, external person, separated from their own inner object world and in this way, can get out of their imagined omnipotent control. Through this process the client can begin to let go of the idealization and instead, build up a more realistic picture of self and other (Winnicott, 1947).

Through the processes of metabolizing and detoxifying in *holding* (Winnicott, 1958) and *containment* (Bion, 1967b), the client's hateful projections are modified and transformed in such a way that he can more readily reintroject them. The therapist gradually works their way back to their own centre of emotions and reflections, and thereby again is able to *respond* and not just *react* to the client's hate (Gabbard & Wilkinson, 1994). The treatment frame is of great importance for clients who function at a regressive level. Through the interaction between therapist and client, a shared common transitional space can be established which can be a basis for the client's ability to internalise the holding functions the therapist has carried out (Winnicott, 1947). In this way the therapist's ability to tolerate the client's intensely hateful feelings may, in itself, produce change in the client.

In order to mobilize the client's self-observation, it is important for the therapist to focus on interpretations which can help the client to become aware that there is a powerful *force* at work inside him which prevents him from observing and acknowledging what is going on in his inner and outer world (Rosenfeld, 1987). Consider for example, the hateful, destructive force by which persuasion and suggestion exert a powerful influence over the client. This force either assumes the role of an adviser or becomes extremely threatening and critical, maintaining the client's delusional way of being in power (ibid.). Interpretations focusing on the dominating split-off parts of self and objects, not only on the bad and destructive aspects but especially on the good and more loving aspects, may help him to deal with this in a less guilty way and so bring along more self-acceptance. This needs to be combined with focus on the force at work inside the client, something he does not deliberately do.

The client can, as Winnicott (1947) has pointed out, only tolerate his own hate if the therapist can hate him. It seems to be important for some clients to experience the hate of the therapist, which means that in one way or another, we need to communicate our hate to our clients. When the hateful feelings are at their most intense, and when the analytic work functions at a regressed level where words are not reliable ways of communicating, the problem for the therapist is how their hate can be communicated to the client without gross countertransference acting out, and without the client misunderstanding their words. At this regressed transference level, interpretations will be misinterpreted and misunderstood and are often experienced by the client as interfering, cruel and hostile. At this point interpretations can be dangerous; the therapist must wisely wait until this regressed and destructive phase is over and emotions have cooled off before clarifying to the client what was going on when they were full of hate and attacking both therapist and therapy (Balint, 1951, 1968; Gabbard, 1996; Gabbard & Wilkinson, 1994; Winnicott, 1947).

The hateful client is functioning at a regressed level where words are not sufficient, and where it is exactly the *repeated experience* in the therapeutic setting of the therapist surviving the hateful attacks and the *non-verbal communication* between them, the client and the therapist, which has a healing and integrating effect on their ability to believe in the stability and power of goodness.

Balint (1951) points out that with regressed clients, it may be a more important task in some periods of the treatment, to *establish and maintain a well-functioning relationship* than to make interpretations, even though these are correct. Balint sees regression as a request or need for a special kind of object relation, and the therapist must therefore to some extent, be willing to let themselves be used by the client in a two-person relationship which cannot and does not have to be expressed in words, but which sometimes shows in a kind of acting-out in the therapeutic situation. The therapist must create an atmosphere where they and the client can tolerate regression in a shared experience, bearing in mind that the therapist's tolerance of hateful acting-out must be without masochistic submission to the client's hateful transference. At the same time, the therapist must be working to establish a triangular relationship in which the client can begin to see themselves from a more mature position (Balint, 1968).

Hate draws the client and the therapist into a *passionate connection*, as Bollas and Mann put it. In therapy with hateful clients who are not able or ready to receive the therapist's "love", and where the therapist inevitably experiences hate, the only connection that will initially establish a genuine relationship is a connection through hate. The important part is therefore the therapist's willingness to come to terms with the extent of their hate and to be prepared to hate the client with a view to doing as little harm as possible, hopefully even doing some good (Mann, 2006). It is hoped that this kind of non-destructive hating is new to the client and gradually has a mitigating effect on their inner world.

Bollas talks of *"loving hate"*. He says that "there are certain persons who feel that until the therapist can hate them, and until they can see evidence of such hate evoked in the therapist, there is a risk that they will never have been known. It is through hate evoked in the therapist, that this kind of person seeks to achieve his sort of intimacy with her. It is when the therapist's steady state of mind and even temper, break down under the weight of the client's negativity that the client takes hope for it is there, in that moment when he sees the therapist's hesitation or senses her frustration, that he feels himself connected to the therapist. In that state there is a sense of merger with the therapist, whose even-mindedness until then, even when she is being empathic and sympathetic, has felt like a refusal, a rebuff" (Bollas, 1985, p. 231).

Mann talks of *"hating-love"*. He says that the therapist is not restraining their hate. Rather, what is restrained is the therapist's desire to act destructively with their hate. Being less destructive than the client, the therapist may be in a better position to begin doing something constructive and creative and finding some love and understanding for the client. The task is for the therapist to contain the hate in a loving way and for the client to experience a less destructive hate with an integration of love and hate or, good and bad. In this way it can be hoped that a more loving relationship can be developed (2006).

> *S is the client I mentioned before who has been paranoid and very hateful. She said that one of the important things that had helped her in therapy was the times when the therapist had scolded her, so letting her understand that there was a limit to what she would put up with; that S had to behave in order to stay in the therapeutic relationship. Even though the therapist never actually did scold her, she never doubted when she was angry and furious with her, signalling that enough was enough. S could tell by her voice, the expression on her face, the words she used and the look in her eyes. Sensing this hate had made her feel that the therapist was affected by her and that she finally had gained access to the real person and not just the false therapist role. This, as well as the therapist's insistance on always going into the hateful transference, gave her a feeling of being important as a person. As she said: "You get paid for saying all the therapeutic crap, but you don`t get paid for being emotionally affected by me".*

It has become clear to me that in therapy, there is an ongoing communication between these clients and the therapists about hate, and that this communication mainly takes place at a non-verbal level, which includes the therapist's non-verbal self-disclosure. Clients sense their therapists' mood, and it would be naive to think that they do not sense hate in their therapists. Keeping the importance of an authentic, honest therapeutic relationship in mind, it is crucial that the therapist is able to communicate their hate when this is required and demanded from the client. It is therefore necessary that the therapist makes a limited self-disclosure of their countertransference with the one and only purpose to increase the client's understanding of their inner world and interpersonal relationships with others. A real and honest communication of emotions in the here-and-now can be crucial in the development and maintenance of a therapeutic alliance with the client. The timing is of great importance because clients functioning at a regressed level are not always ready for the therapist's verbal communication of counter-transference, and therefore must be dealt with, with great delicacy.

When powerful projective identifications take place and create an almost hypnotic atmosphere, "the analyst's capacity to function therapeutically and to contain the situation depends upon his emotional resources and his theoretical understanding. It is important to realize that the two interact together, so that the analyst's emotional capacities can help him to empathize with what is happening and his theoretical conceptual capacity can help him to bear the emotions" (Rosenfeld, 1987, p. 191).

So why do many therapists seemingly not work with hate?

I think it is necessary to accept that in therapy, the playful, symbolic space inevitably collapses for shorter or longer periods of time with these hateful clients who function at a more regressed level. The therapist must be able to contain the client's hateful projections with as little acting out of their counter-transference as possible. The task here is to survive these hateful attacks and still maintain a therapeutic relationship and a neutral position. The therapist must at times be content with fulfilling this task, hoping that the client will be able to believe in goodness, and that this can have a mitigating effect on their hate in that love can begin to develop from hate.

Some clients stop therapy before they really get to work with their hateful inner fantasies and object relations. This may be due to the fact that their therapists are not able to meet them sufficiently in this hateful universe. It is a major challenge for therapists, and it requires courage to authentically meet their clients in what is experienced as the most dangerous and anxiety-provoking place.

It is my experience that we are far too reluctant and anxious to share our hateful experiences with one another, thus preventing us from the benefits of exploring our thoughts. In my opinion, we talk far too little about hate in our clients and in ourselves, and I believe that supervision taking place in a secure and playful atmosphere is of immense importance in order to deal better with the complex aspects of hate described in this article.

CHAPTER FOUR

Survival and helplessness in empty space[1]

Liselotte Grünbaum

In psychotherapy with recurrently traumatised children, I have often felt that sooner or later, what developed in the therapeutic space was an empty, dead atmosphere in which endless nothingness seemed to build up. What develops is an oppressive silence, only to be broken at certain points by a powerful urge to repeat seemingly meaningless fragments of behaviour. While still struggling to contain the temptation to curtail this deadlock, experience tells me that on the contrary, my task is to keep up reverie while waiting for the child themselves to make a move. Thus, in time, the child eventually will say or do something that links between on the one hand the deadness and compulsion to repeat, and on the other hand, the restitution of symbolic thoughts related to the object relations of the inner world. In the following I will try to elucidate this, partly from a conceptual point of view, and partly from my experience in psychotherapy with a 6-year old girl.

---

[1]The present article is a revised version of Grünbaum (2006).

Trauma-related inhibition of symbol formation

Both in developmental research and psychoanalytic practice, there is unanimous agreement that the repeated experience in childhood of intra- and extra-familial violence, as for instance related to war, organised violence, torture, as well as mental or physical abuse and deprivation, may have severe consequences for the developing personality of the child. It is also agreed that in later childhood or in adulthood, the memory of recurrent traumatic experience is not necessarily present in mental space as conscious, verbal knowledge, but may rather be present as disturbing tendencies, to frozen or dissociated mental states and fragmented patterns of actions (Fonagy et al., 2002; Kaplan, 2006; Pynoos et al., 1995; Terr, 1991a, 1991b). While the children and their families are often painfully aware of how these tendencies strain the child's relationships and development, the connection between traumatic experience and the compulsion to repeat may have been lost completely.

Recurrent trauma link together overwhelmed inner states with repeatedly occurring outer events that the child's ego cannot process and integrate in the stream of development. In psychotherapy with recurrently traumatised children, I have repeatedly encountered the need for a type of thinking that may function as an integrating link between the following tendencies: passive, pessimistic attitudes, compulsive repetition, silent states apparently devoid of symbolic thinking and fragmented traces of early, developmental fantasy. Inspired by a recent paper by Mitrani (2007), my assumption is that the mechanisms behind this specific pattern may be related to changes in the developing ego of the child and related to the formation of an unconscious, defensive organisation of object relations based on a premature identification with traumatising objects.

I will take as my starting point the psychological meaning of the traumatic moment itself. This moment is often described as an experience of violent turmoil, in which chaotic fear and anxiety, mental and maybe physical paralysation and confused emotional flooding are predominant. I assume this state to have its counterpart in a violent inner interruption of unconscious, developmental phantasy, or, stated in another way, in a sudden collapse of the child's inner ability to link with containing objects. The resulting inner situation may be compared to the experience of a void or abyss, in which any emotional meaning and thinking is destroyed, together with the ability to form object-related symbols and phantasy.

Experience tells me that in the course of therapy, this inner situation may eventually surface in the child's drawings and play, such as in images relating to endless, dried up deserts, bottomless abysses swallowing up all living creatures or, even worse, disjointed, fragmented drawings in which nothing is linked meaningfully together. However, at the beginning of therapy with a recurrently traumatised child, what dawns on the mind of the therapist when observing the child is rather a diffuse break or annihilation in both the will to live and in living object-related symbolism. In line with this understanding, Tarantelli (2003) has described the mental effect of catastrophic trauma as a "radical break in being which disarticulates the psyche" (p. 915).

If the child, in relation to his parents, repeatedly experiences such a sudden disarticulation of their mental life, one may assume that the survival of the child's psychic life demands radical defensive operations that to some degree, mend the gap between child and parent and at the same time, more or less cancel out the awareness of the catastrophic state. In the early days of psychoanalysis, such a defensive process was suggested by Freud, who described the disavowal of a traumatising outer reality to bring in its wake a splitting of the ego that increases as time goes on (Freud 1940 [1938]). The consequences for the child's further development may be assumed to be a weakening of the ego's synthesising powers, in which the opposing forces between the disavowal and the recognition of the traumatic reality are at the core. Thinking of recurrent trauma as linked to continuous defensive processes was also implied first by Anna Freud and later by Leonore Terr (Freud, 1964; Terr, 1991a). Both noted that if overwhelming events are often experienced, this repetition cannot be altogether unforeseen to the child, meaning that the recurrently traumatised child to some degree will have to protect himself by adaptation to trauma as a way of life, for instance by the development of a perspective on life that anticipates future traumatic experience.

The link to infantile, developmental fantasy was suggested by Melanie Klein in her early paper "Symbol-formation in Ego-development" (1930). Klein suggested that traumatic overwhelming of the infant's mind may occur if the normally occurring, early anxiety-situations related to fantasized attacks on the objects cannot be sufficiently mitigated in the mother-child dyad. She further proposed that to protect himself, the infant is forced to cope prematurely with the resulting anxiety, which may lead to a development of defence mechanisms that will impede the child's capacity for symbol-formation. Thus Klein believed that normal, early aggression and the related fantasies entail an overwhelming anxiety that sets in motion powerful, primitive defences directed towards two sources of danger, namely the child's own aggressive feelings and the attacked object. In relation to the child's own aggressive feelings, the defences imply attempts through evacuation to free the mind of the aggressive feelings. In relation to the object, the defences imply an increased anxiety related to the destruction both of what may so far have been introjected good part-object relations, depressive concerns, and of the survival of the self, because the child comes to fear retaliation from the attacked object; persecutory anxiety. Klein thought that in normal development, this anxiety sets in motion processes of identification and symbolic equation, which in turn lead to both symbolism and the child's relation to reality. However, if the child's early ego capacities and/or the mother's capacity for empathic, loving care do not contain and mitigate the anxiety to a sufficient degree, the result may be the development of precocious empathy and identification with a damaged object. As a consequence, an inhibition may arise in the ego and thwart the child's ability to feel his own aggressive emotions, the inquiring, exploring part of his mind and the unconscious fantasy life; in short an inhibition of symbol-formation.

In the model of the relation container-contained, Bion (1962a, 1962b) further developed the link between overwhelmed inner states of the infant and the containing capacities of the object. Using Bion's terms, a catastrophic inner situation may be understood as relating to a collapse of the relation container-contained. The terror released by trauma can then be thought of as similar to the nameless dread of an infant in relation to an object, such as an outer parent and/or the mental apparatus of the infant himself, which is unable through containment, the processes of reverie, transformation, and interpretation[2], to sufficiently modify its acute fear of dying.

---

[2]In connection with this, interpretation does not necessarily refer to any verbal statement but rather to the mother's ability in her own mind to translate and symbolically understand her child's emotion and accordingly communicate emotionally and take appropriate action to relieve the child's condition.

In an environmental situation dominated by powerful collective violence and expulsion, trauma and the hardship of real life may continuously undermine the mother's emotional capacities, and her difficulties in providing stable containment of her infant is easily understandable. In the wake of societal violence follows danger, fear and deprivation, leading to a catastrophic inner situation that affects not only the mother but also her infant. Thus, what may occur between mother and child can be thought of as an endless repetition in the couple of a vicious circle related to the nameless dread of an infant in relation to an object, which recurrently is rendered unable sufficiently to modify both her and the infant's acute fear of dying. This leaves the child with no other choice than to re-introject not only its own fear of dying, but also the destructive relation to an overwhelmed, unempathic, unhelpful, and at times maybe actively depriving and abusing part-object. The seriousness of this at the same time inner and relational situation, becomes even worse as the child has to go on continuously evacuating its dread by reinforced splitting and projective identification. As this evil circle goes on and on, the child's mental life becomes more and more fragmented and denuded, and consequently it becomes harder and harder both for its inner objects and for its outer parents to provide sufficient and relevant containment.

Living through periods of war, persecution and trauma, the child, and no less his parents, have to find ways both mentally and emotionally, to survive a more or less permanent inner situation in which the self is recurrently flooded by objects felt to be unavailable, fatally damaged and overwhelmingly vulnerable. To return to the Kleinian perspective on premature ego development, I understand this situation to set in motion a kind of premature ego development in which the child's mental apparatus to the best of his ability, is forced to develop in such a way that some form of peace is restored in the inner world.

My proposition therefore, is that recurrent trauma in early childhood may produce changes in the ego of the child which are best understood as a kind of *precocious, developmental adaptation* to an unavailable object and a chronic state of nameless dread. Or, in other words, the child develops a subjective survival strategy that implies a *dualistic unconscious intention*:

a. It is directed towards the inner world and may as such be thought of as *a defensive strategy* that aims to reduce or modify the traumatic fear of dying by minimizing the risk of further traumatic disruption of object-relations, for instance by the shutting down of symbolic functioning and identifying closely with a vulnerable, damaged object.

b. At the same time, it is directed outwards as *a strategy for adjustment to a threatening environment*. As such it aims for protection by reducing the risk of further attacks from real, external figures, for instance by curbing and modulating any passion relating both to loving and hateful feelings.

Through such survival-related forms of adaptation, the child may enter into a state of inner rest that probably may best be described as a paradigm of primitive flight. In the inner world, peace may reign however, the ability for symbol formation is fragmented and debilitated. Because of the resulting weakening of reality testing and the ability for relational thinking, the traumatised child pays a high developmental price, missing out on the social and emotional experience necessary for personality development. Furthermore, the inner rest thus gained is fragile and easily breaks down to be succeeded by survival related anxiety, confusion, and compulsive repetition. In such moments, the child in psychotherapy unconsciously communicates states of lifelessness and despair, often accompanied by an enactment in the transference of subjective, unlinked fragments of the traumatising, past relationships. These fragments may be more or less unobserved by the child but are there to be seen, if the therapist is able to open her mind to introject and resonate with the projected parts of the child's inner world.

Similarity may be found between this conception of the psychological consequences of severe, recurrent traumatisation in early childhood and the psychic organisation that Steiner named "psychic retreat" (1993). By this he described a borderline propensity for withdrawal from depressive and paranoid anxieties into a private, inner sanctuary, a kind of peaceful refuge in which an autistic fantasy of protected rest may be upheld. Working with traumatised children may offer a possibility to witness how such a tendency for retreat may come into being. However, one also has to take into consideration the complexity of a developmental situation in which some parts of the traumatised child's personality follow an ordinary course of development, while other parts seem locked in a perpetual struggle between the dialectic forces of trauma that are the opposite tendencies of avoidance, flight into retreat, and remembering, unrelated repetition compulsion.

Continuing being a therapist in empty space

In my experience, sooner or later the therapeutic process with a severely traumatised child must come to a standstill; first experienced in the countertransference either as a blockage of my ability for reverie or, as an increasing awareness of nothingness in the atmosphere of the playroom. Whichever comes first, it leads to the thought that therapy has reached a deadlock in which movement is impossible and the dialogue with the child impoverished, fixed, or without any consequence. It is like a feeling of something withering away, while empty islands are spreading out both in the child's play and in the relationship. While still in activity with something resembling play, the child apparently has stopped using the playthings for symbolic communication and moved into a locked position, dominated by alert, watchful passivity. In this passive state, a powerful tendency for endless repetition of self soothing, sensorial activities may appear, such as touching and rubbing sand between the hands, taking playthings apart and reducing them to fragments, seemingly without conscious intent, rubbing parts of the body and even activities akin to the deprived infant's tendency to keep himself together by rhythmic rocking in the cradle.

While the child increasingly seems to give up symbolic communication, in the countertransference, I become alarmed by the awareness of a resounding, absolute stillness, both in the playroom and in my own inner world. This may suddenly be interrupted by somatopsychic irritability, states coloured by acute paranoid anxiety, sleepiness or other forms of self-absorption that momentarily compromise my ability to function as a containing therapist.

Repetition as meaningless interruptions of play

The described emptiness is however, only one among other characteristics in therapy with recurrently traumatised children. It is not a total standstill, but rather occurs as interruptions of the ongoing relationship and play of the child. Accordingly, in order to understand what happens in the moments of interruption, it is also necessary to link emptiness to its context, that is to the preceding and following sequences of play and therapeutic dialogue.

It has long been generally acknowledged that in many ways and at many levels, the play of traumatised children will be coloured and formed by the traumatising experience (Terr, 1991a). This also holds true for recurrently traumatised children in psychotherapy. However, more often than not, these children's ability for symbolic play is hampered or disturbed. The therapist may from the very start, be confronted with a very passive child, unable to move in the playroom or, at other times, may meet with a quite manic child, whose feeling of security seems to depend on frantic activity. This activity may resemble play but its motivation does not stem from the need for creative exploration, rather from a need to be in control of unpredictable or unavailable objects.

Play and other forms of creative action presuppose both symbol formation and an ability to maintain a certain permeability of the barrier between inner fantasy and outer reality without a collapse of differentiation. In this way an explorative space in between inner fantasy and outer reality becomes available for play (Caper, 1996; Winnicott, 1971). Assuming trauma to produce a collapse of the exploratory space needed to keep up a playful state of mind, one may assume a simultaneous breakdown of the child's ability to differentiate between inner fantasy and outer reality. In other words, the recurring interruptions in play may probably best be thought of as the child's micro-reliving of infringement and assault in the traumatic moment, popping up uninvited in the fantasy of the child and merging with straying fragments of the normally unconscious, developmentally related, infantile scenarios. Thus, I assume that in split seconds, bits and pieces of traumatic experience and unconscious fantasy become manifest in the consciousness of the child, which means that playing in itself becomes dangerous and frightening. A contributing factor probably is that recurrently traumatised children very often have suffered abuse, which by its very nature possessed a striking similarity to the subjective metaphors of unconscious fantasy. This may render the interruptions to playing especially powerful as, for instance, traces of sexual and physical abuse strongly resound in these moments with pre-existing, unconscious emotions and fantasies of love and hate in relation to the inner and outer parents.

From this perspective, my hypothesis is that inhibition and disturbance of the recurrently traumatised child's ability to play occur because the play is suddenly felt to become much too real. As described elsewhere, the same psychic mechanism is probably at stake in post-traumatic disturbances involving the ability to dream, such as with the post-traumatic nightmare (Grünbaum, 2001, 2010).

Repetition as reliving the traumatic interruption

As described, the play of recurrently traumatised children often encloses merged and chaotic combinations of periods of symbolic play and sudden interruptions, either by stereotyped repetitions or by certain moments or periods, where any liveliness, relating and movement seem to disintegrate and come to a halt. I will now take a closer look at the characteristics of the compulsion to repeat the traces of traumatic experience in enacted behaviour.

Recurrently traumatised children have a salient tendency to adapt to even very disturbing symptoms, conceptualising these as an ego-syntonic part of normal life. Thus, most often in later childhood, they may appear quite unaware of any link between the compulsion to repeat and the earlier traumatising circumstances of life. In therapy, they may blankly reject the existence of repetition, although clearly observed by the therapist, or, while recognising the reality of the repeated action itself, they may shrug this off as an accidental occurrence, something normal that may happen to anybody. Only rarely will such children view the tendency to repeat as a specific event that signifies a frightening interruption to their going on being. In my experience, at this point a verbal interpretation linking trauma to repetition in the transference will have no meaning whatsoever for the child, and the effect will be merely to increase survival strategies and defensive adaptation. This seems to be especially important when dealing with psychosocially disadvantaged children and their families, as with many traumatised refugees, who in order to get relief, have had to tell their story of traumatisation a huge number of times to societal authorities and other officials without getting adequate psychological help. Thus the narrative of traumatisation may in itself have become a survival related repetition, in which the aim of gaining access to concrete relief overpowers any other emotional meaning. In such a context, the therapist's verbal recognition of the other emotional meanings inherent in the story, may not resonate emotionally in the minds of the child and its family, but rather will be taken as confirmation that the unconscious strategies of survival demand that the by now, emotionally empty story, be repeated over and over again. I am in agreement here with Lanyado who emphasizes the importance of the therapist's ability to allow herself and her patient a mutual state of quiet, sympathetic observation (2003, this volume).

At the beginning of therapy, the concrete, enacted repetition may appear and disappear in split seconds, and in such a subdued form that the therapist may doubt her own perception. I have, for instance, repeatedly found myself wondering whether my perception of what happened in a few moments was realistic or, if my sense of reality and ability for empathic reverie had become disturbed and biased by the pain inherent in the anamnestic narrative received from the parents. In my experience, this sudden doubt about my own sense of reality only occurs with patients suffering either from psychotic disturbances or from man-made traumatic assault. I believe that this countertransference confusion reflects at a very concrete experiential level, the common phrase "I don't believe my own eyes". It may be related to an unconscious resonance in the mind of the therapist of the traumatic loss of control and related feelings of utter estrangement, depersonalisation, and confusion. As the therapeutic process proceeds, the dissociative nature of the repetitions and interruptions becomes more explicit, both in the actions of the child and in the countertransference of the therapist who, for instance, may momentarily experience a specific sort of mental paralysis and confusion. This phenomenon seems to take on a specific immediacy and intensity in play psychotherapy, probably related to the above-described characteristic; increased permeability of the differentiation between inner and outer reality in play.

I have come to think of these repetitions as a form of reliving the traumatic interruption in the child's going-on being. Accordingly, I understand the interruption as an urgent, desperate communication of an unthinkable inner space, at the same time empty and flooded with fragmented, bizarre object relations. I believe that only through such meaningless repetition and sudden standstill, is the child able to tell us about the relentlessly continuing traumatic interruption of emotional objects relating in the inner world. From this perspective, one may understand the enactment of interruption and compulsion to repeat as communicating the child's desperate attempts to contain, cope and render bearable the continuing presence of traumatic interruption in the mental life.

In accordance with a Kleinian conception of the transference relationship, these micro interruptions and repetitions, in my view, must be considered an embedded part of the continuing relationship and thought about as such (Joseph, 1985). In time, the repeated enactments may, in very concrete and simplistic ways, come to embed traces of fantasies and feelings relating both to the therapeutic here and now, and to such past and present relationships as are actualised in the relationship. Their subjective qualities become overdetermined in the process, taking on shifting emotional colouring and minute characteristics inside the immediacy of the therapeutic relation. Thus, while playing or not-playing tend to take turns in the therapeutic process, the enacted repetitions of the child more and more seem to pick out exactly those dimensions of traumatic experience that resound both with feelings related to the therapist, the parents, or other important figures in the present life of the child, and with damaged object relations in urgent need of repair (Grünbaum, 2001, 2010). In a more schematic way:

a. The repeated enactments point backwards to traumatising experiences and relationships in the developmental past of the child.
b. The repeated enactments point to the inside of therapeutic space, towards transference related feelings and fantasies.
c. The repeated enactments point outside and forwards, towards present and future strains and worries in everyday life, for instance, related to the family and school.

Strategies for survival in therapeutic space

Recurrently traumatised children may, for whole developmental periods of their lives, have been subjected to traumatic relations and more often than not, have also experienced repeated losses. In accordance with unconscious expectations of unavailable or abusing objects, they usually enter therapy with comprehension. Such children use much energy to keep in control, at the same time trying with all their might to fulfil what expectations they, in projected fantasy, believe the therapist to harbour. Some children, in a more or less artificial or desperate manner, try to appease their therapist, as if it is necessary to hold her together to prevent a traumatic flooding of the self by her uncontained feelings. Other children take the opposite position and seem by actions to convey, "just see how awful everybody thinks I am", whereupon they make a vehement effort to convince the therapist that this is the only truth to be found. Some children present a mixture of both attitudes.

In accordance with Mitrani's technical considerations concerning premature ego development in adults, I have found it very important to take neither the artificial sweetness nor aggressive enactment at their antisocial face value (Mitrani, 2007). Very seldom have I encountered a repeatedly traumatised child who was able to keep up a conscious, goal directed shamming of either good or bad intentions. I rather consider these attitudes to be the result of unconscious, panic-stricken attempts to cope with the compulsion that survival depends on submission-adaptation or fight-flight in relation to unstable, unavailable, sometimes directly terrorizing inner objects. Thus the therapist, together with these children, may discover that even the child's most terrible behaviour, may not give rise to the expected anger and contempt in their countertransference, but rather produce raw and nearly unbearable, mixed feelings of sympathetic resonance, resounding powerlessness and despair. Sometimes these feelings manifest themselves in such a diffuse way, like floating in the air, that the therapist may experience considerable difficulties in localising their origin, for instance whether they belong to the inner world of the child or to themselves. Later in the course of therapy, I have found this constellation of countertransference feelings to be quite a reliable indicator that the child in that moment, is under the sway of fantasies and feelings related to continuing destruction of every possibility for linking with good objects in the inner world.

In line with a Kleinian perspective, I assume that the powerless despair experienced in the countertransference, may result both from the therapist's introjective identification with empty and flooded spaces in the child's inner world, and from their instinctive aversion against identification with traumatising object relations (Bell, 2001; Bion, 1959; Garland, 1998; O'Shaughnessy, 1981). Consequently, I consider the transferential attitude and enacted repetitions of the traumatised child to be a communication that he needs the therapeutic relationship in order to repair and re-introject damaged object relations.

Beginnings are especially important in therapy with these children who sometimes, in what is felt as an endless starting period, evacuate fundamental feelings of terror and confusion. Meltzer metaphorically termed this kind of transference relationship a *"toilet-breast relation"* (1967). This term is apt in calling forth images relating to the conception that recurrently traumatised and deprived children at times need the therapist to function as an undemanding container, willing and able in their own mind to receive and transform unbearable psychic "trash" that the child himself cannot make sense of. In my view, this takes time, and over-hasty attempts to give back the projected material do not further the child's self understanding. Rather, the therapeutic relation will carry the process forward to another necessary step that may include periods of silence and standstill in which very little seems to move in the therapeutic space. This does not generally mean a total stop to play and dialogue, but rather that the periodic interruptions to playing and talking become more frequent and of longer duration.

A clinical case—Laila[3]

Laila was 6 years old when she was referred for child psychotherapy on account of frequent fits of rage, sleep difficulties, nightmares, and severe separation anxiety. According to her mother, Laila could do nothing alone, ambivalently clinging and controlling every movement of the mother. During fits of rage, she pulled her hair out in lumps and grew bodily rigid. She acted in a rough and cruel way towards her little brother but at school she was shy, keeping much to herself. Although no doubt a bright child, she was quite slow in learning Danish.

Regarding her family background and early development, her mother told me that she, Laila, and the little brother, had arrived

---

[3]Parts of the clinical material presented here have published before (Grünbaum, 1997). For reasons of anonymity only information concerning family background that in my experience is common to a great many traumatised refugee children and their families has been included, while more specific information concerning the background has been changed or left out.

in Denmark from the Middle East when Laila and her little brother were 3½ and 1½ years old respectively. The early life of Laila and her parents had been strained by conditions of war, governmental persecution and chronic danger to life. The mother had been imprisoned and tortured some years before Laila's birth. Her father was dead, executed by government authorities in their country of origin. This country had been at war since Laila was 1½ years old and, as a consequence, she and her parents had experienced air-raids and scarcity of food and other supplies. When Laila was an infant, her parents lived in constant fear of their lives due to political persecution. They frequently had to present themselves at the police station for interrogation and several times their house was violently searched by soldiers in Laila's presence.

According to the mother, the early relationship between herself and her baby Laila was quite difficult, the mother being in a fearful and depressed state and Laila crying so persistently that the mother, in despair, would beat her and leave her alone. Laila had from infancy become especially attached to her father, who considered her the apple of his eye.

When Laila was 2 years old, the father was imprisoned and severely tortured. On his release from prison, the parents decided that mother and children had to leave the country. The mother described an emotionally, highly intense farewell scene with the father, half mad with fear and sorrow, desperately kissing Laila's feet over and over again, crying violently and pulling out his hair. The 3-year-old Laila never saw her father again.

After their arrival in Denmark, mother and children lived for 2 years in a refugee-centre before asylum was granted. During this period, the torture related sufferings of the mother increased severely and she became more and more depressed. At the assessment interview, with obvious sorrow and guilt, she told how she would oscillate between preoccupied withdrawal and fits of rage during which she would beat the children severely, especially Laila.

Laila reacted violently to even the slightest mention of her father, for which reason the family had stopped talking about him entirely in her presence. The father's death was kept a secret from the children until Laila was 5 years old. Before the start of therapy, the mother warned me not to mention the father, as she was certain Laila would refuse to see me again.

The setting for therapy: This took place twice weekly for over 2 years. In the same period, the mother was in therapy at a centre for traumatised refugees. I took care myself to co-ordinate meetings with day care institutions and school, and also talked to the mother about once every term, to discuss Laila's development outside therapy.

A speaking silence

From the beginning of therapy, I was struck by Laila's grave and tense facial expression. Most often, she would sit quietly passive, without talking or playing, while appearing intensively to keep track of my eyes, mimic and movements. It was as if she used her eyes to establish a partial contact, the main purpose of which seemed to be a continual visual scanning of my face. At the very start of therapy I felt quite invaded, however in time this changed to the feeling that through her eyes, she tried desperately to hold on to an unpredictable me that without warning, might disappear or else turn against her in sudden rage[4]. Sometimes Laila would try more actively to appease and control me, for instance she brought a sticky little rubber scorpion from home and left it forgotten for several months in her play box. She also brought candies and insistently offered them to me or, equally insistently, wanted me to draw and cut out according to her instructions. My understanding of these and similar behaviours, was that she was confident enough tentatively to test my ability to contain and survive her poisonous feelings, the scorpion, while at the same time anxiously compelled to keep me busy with predictable tasks, drawings and cuttings, or make sure by good offerings, candy, that I would not suddenly transform myself into a dangerous, raging aggressor.

Laila became more and more preoccupied with her own activities and would draw, cut, glue and paint without stopping. As far as it went, she did produce a lot of possibly symbolic material for

---

[4] This persistent visual scanning of the therapist's face is not uncommon in therapy with severely traumatised or deprived children. I assume it to be a procedural reminiscence of the difficult early relation between mother and child. It may be especially related to the infant's attempts to bring forth vitality, empathic mirroring and confirmation from a depressed and anxious mother, however, the anticipatory fear related to recurrent physical abuse may also be assumed to strengthen this tendency.

me to fasten on to; however, she did not appear happily absorbed in creative activity but rather compulsively keeping herself busy. The relationship between us deteriorated as she would not take any initiative herself and got quite irritated by any verbal comment from me, for instance saying, "I am not yet finished". She worked so hard that at times I felt exhausted on her behalf. Verbal dialogue had from the beginning, been somewhat sparse but by now I felt words to die away completely. As Laila talked less and less, correspondingly I became aware of a resounding silence and emptiness in my own inner world and ability to feel and think. At the same time, I felt a mounting inner urgency to find some way of reaching out to her, and was worried about the risk of the therapy breaking down completely. For long stretches, which seemed to last forever in my countertransference, we were locked in a mutual silence, impossible to break.

In the increasing silence, Laila's compulsive activity gradually ceased. She began for the first time to take time off, just sitting, especially by the sandbox, silently sifting the sand through her fingers. Sometimes she flooded the sand with water, kneading it like dough. These activities apparently gave her some kind of concrete sensory containment and relaxation. She seemed to have found a quite peaceful, but also closed-off retreat, filled up with sensations and devoid of symbolic thought. I was sitting by, equally silent. I kept coming back to the idea that enclosed in her own private space for the first time, Laila might momentarily feel secure, in powerful control to prevent anything unforeseen and therefore dangerous happening[5].

The peaceful atmosphere did not allow for any development and, as time passed, I worried increasingly if, and how this might

---

[5] As already briefly implied (in the preceding footnote), such extensive withdrawal to concrete sensory activity points to a withdrawal into a specific inner part-object relation, probably related to empathic deficits in the early mother-child relationship. Thus early traumatisation and emotional deprivation may leave the infant no other choice than to exploit its own premature resources, bringing forth a tenuous premature ego-development in which the child adheres or clings to a primarily sensuous good object, for instance through the eye (compulsively visual scanning mother's face), the ear (sound) or the skin (skin-to-skin experience like stroking, patting, clinging). In the therapeutic relation, the withdrawal may be thought of as the child's seeking shelter in a secluded fantasy of being with or inside a good object. In other words, I believe sensory withdrawal in the therapeutic space to echo an early strategy of survival by which the child attempts to contain transference related feelings of anxiety and turmoil.

come to an end. Then something began to change, at first by glimpses, then coming more to the front as the atmosphere gradually changed taking on a more desperate and tormented quality. In session after session, Laila would now for instance, take the doll family and silently let the family drown in sand and water without any attempts at rescue. I interpreted this as a metaphoric statement that, while locked in silence, inside she was drowning in her feelings. She seldom used the building blocks but one day produced the following scenario:

> *"Laila builds a compact house, its inner space being filled up by blocks; she says that 'nobody lives there'. Then she builds an addition: two rooms with a narrow, inner space. She says that now there are three rooms, one is the toilet, one is for sleeping, and in the third one may eat. She adds a mother doll, sitting at the toilet, searches her box for a father doll, and is undecided between a boy doll and a soldier figure. She asks my opinion on which to choose. I suggest that she finds it hard to know the difference between children and grownups. She takes both dolls, places the soldier outside the house, looking in through a window, while the boy doll is placed in the bathroom in an averted position, face turned against the wall"[6].*

I took the essential meaning of this to be a dawning ability for symbolic thought and with it, a possibility that in time, Laila might become able to process and think about the traumatised relationships. Thus the depicted scenario may be seen as a metaphorical presentation of a reversed relationship between infant self and object, in which the infant self is at the receiving end of projective identification, containing both her own and the object's needs to evacuate traumatic feelings.

The loss of the father as relived in traumatic repetition compulsion

Silence still the main theme, tiny fragments of play began to occur that seemed to point in the direction of the loss of the father as a

---

[6]This and other extracts of text in quotation marks are quotes from my original process notes of the single therapy sessions.

traumatic main theme. This came more and more to the fore, however, retrospectively, subjective traces had been visible from very
early on, for instance in the figure of the above mentioned toy soldier. She very often included this in her activities, although it was
seldom used for anything except to be regularly placed in the sand
box and just left there to disappear. At the end of sessions, she usually took care to put all the toys back in her play-box, but invariably
left the toy soldier, leaving it for me to retrieve. Paintings of foot-
prints or withering leaves were also frequent, which I took as referring to a theme relating to disappearance and death. Her favourite,
spontaneous comment on the withering leaves was very telling. "*It
is winter, the leaves are falling down*".

Eventually, I got the distinct impression that a dawning recognition of something as yet not specified, was about to surface, but, in
split seconds it would disappear again from her conscious thought.
For instance, she would take the play telephone as if wanting to call
someone, or wanting me to do it. It appeared clearly that she had
a specific recipient person in mind but, as soon as she got the telephone, she became unable to say anything at all. On one occasion
she directly said, "*About something I forgot*".

The fragmented memory of the father seemed hidden in a special
interest in the fairy tale of 'Cinderella'. She told me that she had this
story at home in their own language and brought it for me to see.
She stressed several times that she did not remember the name of
Cinderella, that the other girls in the story are mean to her and that
she has to do all the work in the house. As this theme evolved, it
became possible for me to link the fate of Cinderella to Laila's own
preoccupied business with all kind of tasks, her need to keep herself
busy, while at the same time keeping an eye on me to be sure that
I would not turn angry and mean like the stepmother and stepsis-
ters of Cinderella. Laila immediately reacted to this by telling me
that Cinderella's father was dead. I took this misunderstanding or
slip of memory as a sign of her readiness to acknowledge and contain the reality of the loss of her own father. Accordingly, with some
hesitation, I took the risk of mentioning her father's death. Laila
listened and seemed quiet and thoughtful for a while. Her answer
clearly demonstrates the terrific inner struggle needed to integrate,
contain and think about fragmented bits and pieces of visual and
tactile memories. She said,

"... 'But I can't remember what clothes he wore; he had black hair and black eyes and like small black points here', stroking her own chin, apparently referring to the sensory impression of unshaved skin".

Some time later, I became aware that a theme related to feet in a stereotyped way, was repeated in many of her activities. Many of Laila's drawings conveyed an incomprehensible, frightening quality in relation to feet which were depicted as strangely deformed yet also idealized. In fact, this could be seen in her very first drawing in therapy of a female figure with feet that at the same time, seemed to be flowers and deformed lumps. Laila explained that this was, *"A lady with finery on her head and flowers for feet"*. But it was also, *"A motorway with cars, even if you can't see them, because of the lady standing in front"*. In other, later drawings, the feet were not the same size or colour, or were much too small or big for the figure. Often she accidentally cut off the feet with the scissors, made them almost invisible, or left them out all together.

Laila's preoccupation with feet no doubt was condensed, containing many meanings[7]. However, subjective, emotional recognition seemed to become especially salient, as I linked her preoccupation with feet to the impact of her father kissing her feet over and over again in their traumatic farewell. As therapy proceeded, the concept of feet developed into a central, shared metaphor between us, representing an important link between on the one hand, the traumatic terror of the flooded infantile self, eternally locked together with a scary, damaged object, and on the other hand, more ordinary, early anxieties and fantasies about objects. In Laila's most pained states, she would sometimes equate feet with fantasies of other protruding body parts like the nose and ears:

---

[7]Taken as a metaphor, the concept of feet may assume many developmental and cultural meanings: to be able to walk is a momentous moment in the child's development. In certain undifferentiated states of mind and in unconscious fantasy, feet may be equated with other protruding parts of the body (Tustin, 1986). In the Arabic tradition feet have further consciously recognised meanings, for instance, kissing the feet of someone may be regarded as a sign of submission, and the feet of a woman may have a sexual meaning. The soles of the feet traditionally have been the target of a degrading punishment, used as such in the upbringing of children, however, this same degradation is also to be found across cultures in a common torture method, falanga or bastinado, which suggests links to universal unconscious fantasy (Grünbaum, 2007).

"Laila is holding a rag doll in her arms. She tries repeatedly to push in the doll's nose, feet and ears. While doing this, she is repeatedly mumbling, 'Something I can't remember'. She appears to be in quite a confused state and I cannot establish contact with her."

In this, as well as in the episode described earlier of the play telephone, Laila seemed unconsciously to search for something important that was lost to memory and had to be retrieved. I conceived of this as the resounding of an unconscious need. A need not only to repair but, at an even more basic level, to reassemble the traumatically scattered bits and pieces of good inner images in order to be able to restore in her inner world, good images of, and relationships to, both parents as well as to the parental couple.

After over a year of therapy, at the end of a session for the first time, Laila produced a drawing in which a father figure was clearly represented. She even allowed a mother figure to be present on the same paper, although with no relation between them.

"With some urgency, Laila draws a rabbit with yellow skin wearing a suit and a tie, but with naked feet. She cuts out the 'rabbit father' and glues it to another piece of paper. She says that this is to be 'a book with pictures inside'. Next to the rabbit she draws a woman and says that this is a 'mother rabbit'".

Her preoccupation with feet seemed to reach a peak a fortnight later.

"Laila again starts the session by painting a picture of withering leaves. I suggest that the dead leaves have to do with missing an important person that got lost. Maybe she felt that since the last session part of her had fallen and got lost like the leaves. She is preoccupied for a while with a very long festoon of glazed paper that she has been working on through several sessions. Then she asks me to hang it up between the lights. I suggest that she wants to take up space in my room to assure herself that we cannot be separated from each other. She goes to the play telephone, appears to be in a trance-like state, and urgently demands that I call up, 'Rabbit-father and ask, why he doesn't wear shoes on his feet, and ask him if he eats feet'".

Mourning trauma and loss need
an available outer and inner parent

In the preceding extract of material from the therapy, I wanted to show that behind Laila´s refusal for there to be any mention made of her father, was a disavowal of loss so comprehensive that in the first year of therapy, it was impossible for her to form inner pictures and consequently to feel and think any thoughts about the lost object. She seemed instead to have introjected and identified with fragments of the traumatising farewell scene, on the basis of which a primarily narcissistic identification with the father had come into being. Or, in other words, it was as if she kept the lost father alive in unconscious fantasy, as quite a manic, omnipotent part of her self. This tendency revealed itself for instance, in her behaviour when enraged, pulling out tufts of hair, just as her father did at their final parting. I conceived of her disavowal and consequent identification with the father as the survival strategy of a lonely, bewildered 3 year old child, keeping feelings of abandonment at bay, protecting both herself and the fearful, depressed mother against an uncontainable flooding of depressive feelings. Her omnipotent identification is evidenced quite clearly in this fragment from one of the early sessions.

> "Laila has again, seemingly without intention, left the little soldier buried in the sand. She puts a baby doll high up on the neck of a giraffe and the two of them together trample the mother doll and small animals into the sand. Then she leaves the sandbox to make a call using the toy telephone, but she cannot say anything".

In the second year of therapy, Laila seemed to develop a somewhat better tolerance and containment of separation and related depressive feelings. This was first evidenced in the transference by her repeated building and repair of two separate houses of sand, one for her to live in and one for me. At this time during one of my conversations with her mother, she told me that at home, Laila was less angry but sadder than before, sometimes crying without obvious reason. The mother also told me that before an approaching, planned break from therapy, Laila had reacted violently at home when the mother told her that a near relative had gone away for a while to "live in a camp". According to the mother, Laila immediately broke down in lengthy, disconsolate crying. While trying to comfort her child, the mother experienced intense grief related to the loss of her husband and native country.

I can of course not know for sure what happened inside Laila to elicit this sudden breakdown, although considering the central themes of therapy as described above, Laila's violent grief is probably best understood in the perspective of a sudden traumatic re-experience of loss, most likely related both to the loss of the father and to loss, from early infancy, of the already fragile links to a good mother. It may be that the actual wording of the mother's message, an important relative to "go away to live in a camp", were received in Laila's mind as a critical traumatic reminder both of the intense farewell scene and loss relating to her father, and in the wake of this, the equally shattering experiences during their flight and the asylum centre, together with a severely traumatised and depressed mother.

However, the important thing seems to be the present context, as this time an available, containing object, the mother, was near by, able to share in and help transform the overwhelming feelings of grief. So it was probably no mere random chance that Laila experienced this belated, overwhelming breakdown at home, together with her mother who thanks to her own treatment, was now able to respond with tender care. Or, stated a little differently, in line with Gaensburger's suggestion about early childhood traumatisation and loss, I presume that in this episode, Laila at last succeeded in bringing her feelings of loss in the primary relation to her real, external mother so she could afford to experience and communicate the full force of loss and desolation (Gaensburger, 1995).

Concluding thoughts about psychotherapeutic techniques

Psychoanalytic psychotherapy is about subjective reality, about the inner world, as this has been built up by the mind from life experience and constitutional disposition. Working with trauma-tised clients, adults and children alike, we have no direct access to what happened in the past. The psychotherapeutic discourse does not aim to reach an objective truth hidden behind traumatic symp-toms, but rather aims at restoring and setting free inner forces of integration and relational understanding, and in more general terms, at supporting the re-start of emotional development.

In psychotherapy with children who, through whole developmental periods, sometimes through most of their lives, have suffered recurrent trauma, abuse and neglect, it may be difficult to remember Bion's wise recommendation to put aside memory and desire (Bion, 1967a). The painful feelings conveyed through the narratives of trauma and loss received from parents or foster parents, often supplemented by case file documents, may be difficult to set aside in the mind. No less so because, as already described, recurrent trauma have the power to deprive the psyche of a means of symbolic communication, and in addition set in motion comprehensive defensive processes that further increase a split in the ego between normally unconscious developmental fantasy and the traumatised parts of the personality.

Consequently, the child psychotherapist may be confronted with children not able to communicate, either verbally or through play, their subjective version of inner and outer reality and life history. The resulting powerful silences, to be broken only by senseless repetitions, give rise to painful feelings, difficult to sustain and contain in the countertransference. The therapist may be tempted to fill the void, be it with lifeless interpretations derived from theory or anamnestic information, or be it with concrete suggestions about the often burdensome present everyday life of the child. However, the therapeutic process with these children cannot be rushed. In my experience, the only way to help the ego of the child to regain its synthesising powers is for the therapist to wait patiently while opening her mind to introjective identification with the split emotional reality conveyed by the child through, for instance, recurrent silent states and repetitive actions.

In this work, I have found it helpful to think about the described subjective traces of recurrent trauma as communicating multiple meanings that in time have to be worked through in the transference relationship.

Firstly, the child's way of relating through projective identification communicates the strategies of survival that in the traumatising past, were developed with the dual intent to control and appease unstable or threatening objects while at the same time, diminish anxiety and keep together the child's ability for going on being.

Secondly, while useful in the past, in present life the defensive organisation needed to keep up survival strategies compromises the child's ability for symbol formation, his sense of reality and his ability for relational thinking.

Thirdly, once the therapist has learned through experience how and where to look, the child's movements in the therapeutic space often contain from the outset, tiny glints of fragmented play or action that with hindsight, seem clearly to point towards a repetition of subjectively processed, specific fragments of traumatic memory. I see this as the child's early communication of a need to make the unthinkable thinkable; to enlist the help of the therapist in integrating split off and fragmented traces of traumatic experience.

Finally, to make matters even more complicated, it is my experience that in childhood these fragments of subjective traumatic memory are generally enclosed and fused with also split off fragments of poorly integrated, unconscious infantile feelings and fantasies.

To sum up the more technical points relating to the above conception of what goes on in the mind of the recurrently traumatised child:

1. The therapist has to wait patiently, abstaining from a premature interpretation of the child's survival strategies, but rather allowing the specific pattern to develop in the transference, until what this is about forms in their own mind. Instead of trying eagerly to reach out to the child, it is necessary that the therapist tries to contain and understand their own countertransference feelings and fantasies. In other words, for a long time at the beginning of therapy, the therapist's own feeling states and anxieties may be the main tool for eventually understanding what is going on in the child and in the relationship.

2. At the same time, while waiting, it is also necessary that the therapist patiently keep on trying to reach through survival strategies and make contact with the terrified, unarticulated infant in the child's mind. This may, for instance, relate to feelings of impending catastrophe or deadness that may flood the therapist's own inner world exactly when the child is about to leave the compulsive repetition of survival strategies and in action language, is conveying his inner flooding and emptiness.

3. The therapist's mental processing, reverie, transformation and interpretation, of the subjective meaning and traces of memory implied by senseless repetition, must take its time and partly takes place as an unconscious activity. While early glimmers may have conveyed pointers to be understood, it takes the development of a sufficiently strong transference relationship before these fragments of traumatising object relations in the mind of the therapist, attain the necessary abundance and substance as symbolically invested images and fantasies.

The main point of my argument is related to the risk of the development of a transference relationship that, in some aspects, however partial, may resound and re-enact the traumatising object relations in the inner world of the child. It is my experience as a psychotherapist and supervisor that a crucial dimension in this work is the therapist's ability to contain and transform both the terror of trauma itself and the resulting defensive organisation, built up to protect the child's psyche against future experience of traumatic flooding and collapse. As therapists, we do not need to be in a hurry verbally, to force unwanted split-off parts of inner or outer, present or past reality on the child. Rather, we must take as our point of departure the offer to the child of a benign, meaningful understanding of his here-and-now relationship with the therapist, maybe linking this to the present difficulties the child experiences in life outside the therapeutic space. Once a dialogue like this gets going, the chance is that the relationship to the therapist will evolve into an emotionally alive, intersubjective platform. To have such a secure platform on which to stand is necessary for the child to gain sufficient trust and motivation to consider giving up, or at least modifying, the most disabling aspects of trauma-related survival strategies.

Not until this has developed, will the child really start to communicate about the traumatisation itself. This most often takes place as an unconscious elaboration of the already repeatedly enacted, small enigmatic fragments of play or action as, for instance, evidenced by Laila's repetition of the theme of feet. If this process is given sufficient time and the therapist's careful attention, metaphorical images and manifestations will gradually come into existence, making it possible for the therapist to grasp what subjective meaning the child has unconsciously given to the traumatising events of the past. When it comes to recurrent traumatisation, the first and foremost aim of psychotherapy must be to establish the preconditions for the child to reconstitute, mourn and eventually repair the damaged object relations of inner life. However, considering the extent of the pain and self defeating defences often met with in recurrently traumatised children, it is an open question how far into adolescence and adult age the integration and development brought on by psychotherapy will be maintained.

While sitting together in silence with Laila, I was repeatedly reminded of Edgar Allan Poe's description of the despair and confusion related to impossible attempts to hold on to the good objects threatened by disaster.

> "And I hold within my hand
> Grains of the golden sand –
> How few! Yet how they creep
> Through my fingers to the Deep,
> While I weep – while I weep.
> O God! Can I not grasp
> Them with a tighter clasp?
> Oh God! Can I not save
> One from the pitiless wave?
> Is all that we see or seem
> But a dream within a dream"
> (Poe, 1947: 406)

To me, this poem and especially the lines cited above, poignantly and precisely express the real psychological tragedy of recurrent traumatisation and overwhelming loss, namely the isolated, dream-like experience of desperate, impossible attempts to save the internal objects from continual destruction.

CHAPTER FIVE

The power to play with movement, vibrations and rhythms when language emerges

Chantal Lheureux-Davidse

W hen we meet an autistic child, retreated in his world, we often ask ourselves whether he will start to talk at some point, or whether he will never have access to language. The work of Bick (Williams, 1987) on the observation of babies with their mothers, the studies on pre-natal sound in intrauterine life by Maiello (1997), the research at the Centre National de la Recherche Scientifique (CNRS) on imitation by Nadel (Nadel & Decety, 2002), and exploration of the role of very early shared emotions developed by Trevarthen (1997), give us numerous indicators of the necessary conditions for access to verbal language.

Psychoanalytic research into autism makes us sensitive to the importance of cathecting body image in the relationship with the other, for the development of the corporal ego, and to the role of early fixations and regressive movements in relational development within the context of the transference. Once the child feels himself to exist in his body with some continuity, he feels involved with himself and with others, in a shared communication.

Meltzer (1975), brought to light the movements of cathexis and withdrawal of cathexis in relation to the body, which go together with what he has called the reversibility of sensorial dismantlement.

Indeed, when the autistic child, submerged by an excess of sensations or emotions, cuts himself off from bodily feelings in an attempt to soothe himself, he temporarily breaks the link between psyche and soma in order to take refuge in his thoughts. His thoughts may then drift little by little by resonance, loosing their logical and contextual links. Thus, the sensorial capacity of the child is fragmented; each sense becomes independent of the others and no longer finds a link with them. The child can no longer listen when he looks, and touch is sometimes necessary first before he can have access to the visual impressions. This sensorial dismantlement, while reversible, results from states of sensorial saturation that irrupt and limit the possibility of meeting with the other.

When these organizations with splits have been in place for too long, they deprive the child of the link with his bodily feelings and with his feeling of existing. His corporal ego gets erased and all spontaneous communication with others becomes problematic. The child loses the sense of otherness, and sometimes even physical movement become difficult. Initiating a movement for instance may then become impossible. Experiences of annihilation may arise, as if the body no longer existed. Bodily image gets distorted, as if little by little, extremities are torn off; the hands and the feet, the lower part of the body, the mouth, the axis of the back no longer maintains the body's tonicity and the look is elsewhere. Facial expressions become frozen and all communication seems to become impossible. To fight against the risk of psychic collapse, experienced in the body like a physical collapse, the child tries to maintain itself with a protective muscular shell in that the child tenses up, that acting as a second skin.

To accept these children for psychotherapeutic sessions is often asking too much of psychoanalysts who do not always think that an evolution is possible in these circumstances. How could one meet such a child especially when there is no sign of verbal language, and when pre-verbal language appears non-existent?

But do we need to wait for a baby to speak, before we think of speaking to it? When autistic children do not utter a sound, it is not uncommon that they understand what we say. For some other children without verbal language however, they cannot even bear to listen to other people's words, up to the point that they block their ears with their hands.

The unpredictability of the voice is sometimes unbearable. The predictable rhythms and sounds of music can also be unbearable, especially when the music is sung. How can we facilitate such children meeting the other person when they are so profoundly enclosed in archaic states, even before it is possible to integrate the acoustic and the visual?

Capacity to play on the archaic level

Are the autistic children who are so difficult to access directly when you meet them, also incapable of play? Is the capacity to play reduced to having access to symbolization? The observation of babies with their mothers and clinical experience with autistic children makes us take another view on this question. Have we asked ourselves the right questions about our capacity to play on those levels that concern them? Would meeting autistic children become possible by the metaphoric route?

To avoid a relationship that is too direct and unpredictable, autistic children seek their sensations in the inanimate worlds that they can control. Stereotypes give them access to sensorial qualities that are normally found in a direct relationship.

What is really at stake is our capacity to play with pleasure in archaic sensorial registers so that the child can have its experience of shared play. It is the interest that the therapist takes in these sensorial experiences that are lived by the child, and the fact he recognizes and describes them, which produces a shared experience. This favours the transformation of a sensoriality that hitherto remained unconscious, into jubilation through feeling oneself the author of these sensations. This is a precondition to constructing the feeling of existence.

But how do we find our power to play with autistic children or very handicapped people who are without verbal language? Because of their difficulties, they do not enter into a relationship nor reinforce naturally the narcissism of those around them. If we start from the a priori that every contact already is engaging the other, even before there is verbal language expression by the child, our enlarged sensitivity for the relationship helps us to find the terrain to meet on the very primitive level of the archaic sensoriality.

When we see a child play with the pleasures of repetitive archaic sensoriality in therapy, we realize that this echoes the sensorial and relational experience of the baby in the uterus, even before sensorial differentiation has been established. Thus the experience of movement, vibrations and then rhythms precede, before the 4th month of pregnancy, the experience of sound. Later, after birth, this is accompanied by the visual register and the comments of the mother, and is a pleasure to think of. The *precoces* fixations around the 4th month of pregnancy, or the refuge in these regressive states preceding catastrophic experiences, plunge certain autistic children into unconsciously but actively seeking sensorial experiences linked to these archaic levels. The stereotypic gestures, sounds and words are a witness to this.

When the autistic child is installed in his relational isolation, with his stereotypical and repetitive behaviour, and the therapist remains emotionally and psychically absent, the child often stays in a sensorial register that is inward looking, showing no signs that any language could be possible. It is important to measure the chance that these children offer us to enlarge our consciousness and our sensitivity to contact again these archaic relational experiences. When doing so, we can give them the possibility of sharing, the possibility of playing with our verbal language and finding pleasure in it. It is natural for a mother and father to play with their baby from its birth, and to comment on what the baby feels, even if the baby does not speak back in return. But when the child grows up and becomes more autonomous, this spontaneity of commenting on the life of the child is lost. If it continued, it could even become intrusive. If we join the autistic child in this capacity to play and comment on their interest in seeking this archaic sensoriality, we might be surprised and even marvel at how much improvement is made in their comprehension. They understand what we say, and answers become possible by signs that show a reinvestment of the visual exchange and the tonicity of their body and mouth. In the best cases some sounds emerge or even words, all this achieved through taking pleasure in communicating.

Houdé (1997) has written about the necessity to inhibit our sensorial strategies in order to have access to a more secondary thinking. I would extend the reflection on our difficulties as therapists by highlighting that in the presence of autistic patients, we have often inhibited ourselves when they almost fully navigate in the unconscious sensorial experiences. By finding these experiences again ourselves, through what they show us, we can give words to these sensorial pleasures and transform them into perceptions. Only then does this convey the feeling of existing in the relationship with the other.

In addition to this, if the comments we make are spontaneously coloured by emotions, with feelings of wonder for the capacity to play with two-way communication, the dialogue installs itself more easily and more quickly. The stereotypic behaviour then diminishes, and the language that installs itself in unchangeable categories which cannot be transposed to another context is limited.

Vibrations and the feeling of existing

A group of four autistic children between fifteen and twenty years of age, without language, in deep retreat from the world, has given me clues for my reflection. I was seeing these young people in the context of their group, mostly without any communication, hypotonic, reacting only slightly to the voice.

It was on an autumn day when two gardeners came in to trim the branches of the bushes with a chainsaw. It made a noise like hell.

At that moment, the four youngsters rose and went spontaneously towards the courtyard, attracted by the vibrations of the machines that seemed to wake them up. Side by side, their bodies were more tonic, their faces lit up and became expressive, and they looked and smiled at each other in shared jubilation. However, as soon as the sound of the machines stopped, these young people switched off and seemed to fade, lose all firmness and close themselves up again.

Elise was very lively that day and became joyful. Normally she cried a lot without making a sound, chronically unwell with ENT (Ear, Nose, Throat) troubles, with an ongoing runny nose since birth. Would a meeting become possible for them through the mediation of this shared sensorial experience of vibrations?[1]

---

[1] I had followed a baby that remained fixed in sensorial experiences and vibrations before the integration of the acoustic, because he had spent the last 5 months of pregnancy beside a dead twin in the same womb. After his birth, only the vibrations of his environment reassured him, as well as movements. He fought against sleep to reassure his mother he was well, awake and alive but this exhausted him which caused a great hurdle in his development (Lheureux-Davidse, 2006).

With autistic children who have no language, it is not unusual for tham to react primarily to low sounds which vibrate more than high-pitched ones. Low sounds make the lower part of the body vibrate, while high-pitched sounds make the top of the head vibrate. It is important to appreciate the pleasure of verbal language shared through the vibratory effect of sounds in the body, before it is even a matter of acoustics. During the first babblings, the baby enjoys making his lips vibrate to play with the noisy vibrations that he causes. Similarly, a normally developing baby plays with sounds that make the cavities of his mouth and nose vibrate with 'mmmm' or 'a-reuh'. Moreover, his crying is sometimes transformed into sensorial pleasure at producing sounds, giving way to experimentation with melodies in the form of gurgles.

The baby is more in contact with his mother after his life in the womb if she has a lively, "inhabited" voice. Indeed, a mother who is well in touch with herself will have a more vibrant voice, with anchorage in the low sounds. Her voice will also be more melodic, whereas a depressive mother, who withdraws cathexis from her body, will have a less vibrant voice, as if the voice was speaking from elsewhere, and a more high-pitched tone. The popular expression that relationships make us vibrate should be taken literally.

Playing together with vibrations and variations of the voice

In the clinical material linked with autism, the alternation of high-pitched sounds and low sounds is often directed at a cathexis of the lower part of the body, in an attempt to relate the lower part of the body with the higher part, where there has been a horizontal split in which only the higher part of the body was cathected.

With autistic children, the shared experience of play with vibrations and of play with sounds, low sounds in particular, may be a necessary stage for some, preliminary to the discovery of the pleasure of verbal exchanges: play with vibrations, then with sounds and noises, then with vowels and consonants, with the rhythm of words, low and high-pitched, strongly expressed or whispered.

These experiences with sounds trace directions in the meeting space, from outside to inside, followed by from inside to outside, traces of sensorial communications at the origin of forms.

These vibrations and these sounds, which can be used in different circumstances with slight variations, give an experience of language in an archaic form, but a poetic one at that. It is like a play with words that resonate with other words because of having sounds in common, or identical rhythms, which give pleasure in pronunciation or scansion. Variations with vowels and consonants, in different circumstances, feel like words that can vary in meaning depending on the context in which they are used. When autistic children start to talk, they usually have no problems articulating. Their verbal expression does not, however, always go through the linguistic experiences typical of babies. Complete words, even entire phrases, may suddenly and directly be uttered, without the experience of babbling.

The choice of words used by autistic children is often related to a single context and cannot always be transposed to another. Playing with variations and vibrations may soften this rigidity and thus facilitate access to language, provided that they act at sufficiently archaic levels, so the child does not get confused or sensorially saturated.

The work of Mottron (2004) on the way autistic children listen shows that they have a tendency to focus on details to the detriment of an adjustment between the details and the context as a whole. Each detail becomes a category for them. Thus, autistic children have difficulty accessing the notion of concepts because of the hyper-compartmentalization of every detail. For example, the concept of 'cat' cannot be experienced apart from the real experiences of each cat they have met with. This explains why every single cat, with its particular attributes, becomes a concept of its own. This is why the transposition of one experience to another context remains problematic.

Playing with variations, vibrations and sounds, offers on the contrary, an experience of changing perspectives and contexts. This should support access to verbal language. Furthermore, looking at this from a developmental perspective, the experience the foetus has of vibrations happens prior to the experience of sound at 14 weeks. Indeed the development of the senses and hearing in particular happens in the fourth month of pregnancy.

It seems to me a good idea, in the therapeutic setting, to remain sensitive to the vibratory experiences to which the autistic child reacts, in order to make them an opportunity for a shared meeting with the therapist, when he makes the importance of the vibration explicit.

Dialogue by movement

From the beginning of the 4th month of pregnancy, the foetus in the womb is in dialogue with its mother through alternation of their respective movements. When the mother moves, the foetus stops moving until the mother pauses and her heart rhythm settles and finds its tempo again. The foetus then responds with movements relative to the preceding movements of the mother; it is a real dialogue through this alternation of movement.

Similarly, while autistic children in therapy have not yet become reachable by verbal contact, they may still be very receptive to a relational exchange with the therapist through movements and relocations in space, provided they have the capacity to play with these archaic levels with pleasure. In this way, they prepare an opening for the occurrence of a more elaborate language which in the best of cases can take the form of verbal language.

It is always touching to see how much mothers take delight in every word, every expression or every sound from their baby, commenting every movement or shift, with an a priori that everything is cause for language. Too often, we lose this capacity with people who have great difficulty in relating, like autistic and physically or mentally handicapped people.

The intrusive sound

Meeting with Dorian[2] in therapy, has become possible through these archaic levels. Dorian is a boy of around 10 years. He is physically handicapped, in a wheel chair, his body wrapped from head to toe in a supportive mould. Only his arms and his head can move. His physical handicap is accompanied by severe autism. He has no verbal language. For years he has clung to small "autistic objects", two lids that he kept in his hands. When he lost his vigilance and let the lids drop, he would fall to pieces. He was plunged into a state of

---

[2] The first name and the family name are modified for this presentation.

terror that made him howl until he had them back, which he was not able to do by himself. His muscular stiffness, like a shell, attempts to fight against sensations of bodily collapse but causes intense tensions, even cramps, and ends up being painful. Attempts to implant a pump inside his belly, to release a relaxing fluid into the spinal cord, failed twice. This may be because his system rejected it as relaxation causes such a great fear of collapse. He cannot bear any sound or music. He is overwhelmed by life in his group. States of sensorial saturation prevent him from filtering what comes to him to the point that he seems to dissolve and lose himself in his environment, which he experiences as invasive. He tends to seek release through piercing screams and if he relaxes a moment, he checks his solidity by hitting his jaw with his fist, or biting his hand violently.

Meeting with a psychotherapist on a one to one basis is easier for him, because it limits the unpredictability of his environment. The aim of therapy was for him to be able to relax without fearing he would collapse. This was supported by establishing a relationship in order to provide for the differentiation between external and internal, and for a protective shield to develop.

For some time I named everything that could be attractive, as I would have done with a baby, and Dorian seemed to appreciate this. I used the occasion of pushing his wheelchair from one building to the other on the way to my office, to name the sensorial and aesthetic pleasures that presented themselves, while underlining, sometimes in song, that it was an opportunity to feel quite tranquil and relaxed. Dorian would start to sigh deeply, to which I responded in an alternating rhythm. The word 'tranquil' was a word he spontaneously used several months later during his sessions.

He started to enjoy relaxing by yawning abundantly with deep sighs. But the muscular relaxation would quickly make him anxious to the point that he would hit his jaw violently or bite his hand. I put into words his worry that he would collapse if he relaxed, and his need to verify his solidity by feeling the robustness of his jaw, bones and teeth.

I put close to him, within his grasp, some rubber animals, flexible but firm. By imitating my gestures he could feel their elasticity, soft and solid at the same time. He seemed to appropriate, little by little, these qualities for himself, and started to enjoy a more relaxed state while still feeling solid, without hitting himself anymore.

Sounds of the outside and sounds of the inside

When returning to his group, he would re-discover his anxieties about acoustic invasion and would immediately start to shout or to hit himself. This was also the case during stormy days when the rain hit both the windows and his eardrums very strongly. One day, we heard throbbing machines blowing leaves in the garden. I was afraid that he would again take refuge in his releasing strategies, so I asked him whether he too could make noises, his own noises that spoke of the unpleasant noises outside. He looked me straight in the face and applied himself to produce a new sound voluntarily, "brrrreeeee". I congratulated him and dramatized the idea that the sounds coming from inside him were a way of telling the sounds coming from the outside that they were unpleasant, so that Dorian could push these sounds far away from him. He seemed very reassured by this proposal and went through this experience without shouting or biting himself.

Some days later I learned that, 'Dorian was not well at all at the moment'. I expressed surprise, because I felt exactly the opposite. His project worker said that in the last few days, he had been making a constant, low sound during meals. I was gratified that he had spontaneously been able to apply this technique in a different setting, a place very loud and invasive; the children's dining room. His project worker was reassured when she understood that Dorian was starting to protect himself from outside noises, by realizing a form of language.

He was also re-establishing a solid anchorage with his vertical axis, by joining his hands spontaneously and by alternating movements from left to right with his head, which I supported with an improvised nursery rhyme that beat in rhythm on the theme of left meeting right. Reconnecting the halves of his body around the rediscovered vertical axis, gave him more tonicity without him building a protective shell as he had done before. His look settling little by little, he could lean back with more confidence on the headrest of his chair, normally made for that purpose.

Explorations of space by the tongue, the teeth and the breath

Re-cathecting his verticality behind and in front of him, gave him access to his mouth which was becoming more toned. He was now capable of keeping his lips closed to contain his saliva and to explore some sensations in the cavity of his mouth. I named for him the pleasure of the tongue feeling secure between solid teeth at the moment when uncontrollable movements of the tongue were attempting to find a containing wall to situate itself in space.

The tongue is the first organ for exploration of space, well before the limbs can be used. Research in embryology shows that after one month of pregnancy, the tongue, arms and legs are formed, all at the same time. All these migrate from the same area, the cerebral stem. Thus, the tongue, arms and legs have, by their common origin in the time and space of their formation, common functions in exploring space.

Dorian started to explore the space of his mouth with his tongue, as if he were internalizing the safety he had found again. It allowed him to articulate "ah's" and "oh's", which he accompanied by breathing, as a kind of experiment with the directions of the sound from the inside to the outside of his mouth.

I named all these pleasures with the sounds linked to his breathing. Hearing the word 'breathing', Dorian took a small rubber pig, put it close to his nose in order to smell it and asked, "What is the smell?" followed by, "The pig". He then explored the vibrations coming from the shocks caused by clapping his jaws together. My mind grasped that when I spoke to him about inside, 'dedans' in French, it was for him as if I had said 'deux-dents' in French, 'two teeth' in English. The soft sounds of the breath leaving the mouth could exist in the meeting of the sounds of solid teeth. Metaphorically, I represented to myself that he could exist in the middle of an opening that corresponded to the mouth, in a birth finally soft like a breath, springing from good fantasies of the primal scene, which he could feel through the clapping of his jaws. Dorian was born prematurely and had to undergo more than a month of respiratory assistance in an incubator. His handicap was a consequence of his premature birth.

Dorian then experimented further with soft sounds like 'ya!' and harder sounds that are pronounced with the teeth like, 'tata, mata, ta' which he accompanied with sounds of clicking teeth.

Oral aggressivity and phantasms of the primitive scene

I then thought about the difficulty that Dorian might have in dealing with food that is hard to bite or chew, in relation to his difficulty in bearing aggression. His food was essentially sweet, liquid and mashed, which he tended to suck. This is something one often finds with children stuck in a pre-ambivalent oral phase, before the teeth appear.

At one of the next sessions, I displayed two flexible rubber balls with bumps on them, which he crushed between his hands with pleasure. This made me think of mandibles that crush food with pleasure. He said, "Two balls" and articulated two other words: my first name 'Chantal' and 'Johanna', the trainee psychologist who attended the sessions. I commented to Dorian that all these words, 'Chantal, Johanna, two balls', are really nice to pronounce because in the middle of each of them, is the sound 'a' that seems to feel quite comfortable in the middle. He was jubilant and spontaneously repeated them with pleasure. The 'a' in the middle of the words seems to be in resonance with the vibrations experienced in the centre of the body. He then turned his attention to a rhythmic egg that he placed on his axis saying, "Egg". He passed it from one hand to the other, the same way babies pass a rattle, with a lot of concentration from one hand to the other, experiencing the acoustic vibrations from inside the toy. These alternating movements from left to right facilitate the development of the vertical hinge of the body, connecting the left and right half.

The following session, Dorian repeated perfectly and with pleasure, the word 'Johanna' all the way between his group and the office, in memory of the sound games from the previous session. He seemed to take pleasure in the rhythmic mouthing of the three syllables with the 'a' in the centre of the word. I had the feeling that in the transference, I occupied one of the extremities of the word, while Johanna occupied the other which created a place in the centre for Dorian, represented by the 'a' in the middle.

Dorian played with these three syllables by saying: "Jo-ha-nna, Jo-nna, ha-nna, Jo-ha-nna", with a poetic awareness of the place of each sound, making variations to form other associations of syllables. I had the impression that the 'a' in the middle represented, by resonance, him between his parents, and that with these games he sensed his place and his existence coming from the meeting of his parents, just as he would say, "Jo-nna" taking care not to put the 'a' in the middle.

That day, we walked past several people from the institution, and we played at pronouncing the first names that had three syllables,

'Jo-ha-nna, Jo-na-than'. However, he did not say first names when they did not have the same vowels.

In the session, Dorian continued to explore making *low* sounds vibrate in his throat, alternating them with a chattering of his teeth, sounds of soft vowels and hard consonants. On the way back, we met his physiotherapist Anne-Marie. My enthusiasm authorized me to tell her about the good time we had had pronouncing first names with Dorian. She told me that Dorian had never been able to say more than half of her first name, 'Marie', upon which Dorian responded with, "Anne-Marie", as if now, the two parts could exist simultaneously together and differentiated (Haag, 1985).

Playing with sounds and playing by sharing words

Dorian was looking forward as much as I was, to the next session and the opportunity to play with the sounds of words. We witnessed a real explosion of words that he launched into with great freedom of association during our exchange. This left the three of us very moved.

On the way to the session Dorian was already pronouncing with pleasure, "Jo-ha-nna". When he got into the office, he noticed a crocodile which had movable parts of its body. I opened its mouth and it started to squeal. I said that the crocodile would like to talk, but that he did not know how to; he could only produce funny sounds with his mouth. Dorian immediately attempted to produce sounds with his mouth, while closing his eyes to better feel the vibrations and the placing of the sounds, "a-u-iu, en". Then he got distracted by sounds from a neighbouring bathroom and by the sounds of children passing in the corridor. I asked him whether he too had sounds from inside that speak of the sounds he has heard outside. He responded clearly, "Bathroom" and he then alternated sounds, making them vibrate for the pleasure it gave in the mouth with articulated words that he seemed to choose carefully. "It was long ago, Jo-na-than, a happe-ning, and 'aï-keuill-keuill'" ("il y a- long-temps, Jo-na-than, un é-véne-ment").

In hearing and repeating these associations of words, I noticed a rhythmic pronunciation of three beats in the sounds the words have in common: 'a' and 'en' (refer to the French). I highlighted this to him, and using the same words, sang them with a rhythm.

He continued his improvisation by saying, "ou-an, o-or", followed by "dada". He made me think of a baby immersed in the delight of babbling. I verbalised this saying that it is nice to play with the sounds in the mouth just for fun. He looked at me smiling, shifted his chair a little bit to the left and said, "On the left, the car, tranquil, dada". He then practiced some 'ah's' and 'oh's' that he produced on an out-breath as he had done before. I told him that he always had a great reservoir of sounds and words inside him that one can use to make sounds and words one's whole life, and that there are plenty in stock. He seemed comforted not to have depleted these through talking and he yawned, showing deep relaxation.

He then spontaneously tried the pronunciation of a new letter: 'r'. His language seemed to be more organized. I imitated him and commented on this new pleasure. He followed with other words, "The forest, the road", that contain the letter 'r' in the middle (in French: la forêt, l'autoroute). Johanna added, 'crocodile' to the repertoire of words with an 'r'. Dorian continued saying, "Password, the words" and "broom-broom". We looked for the letters in common between these selected words, and discovered with wonder, that the letters in common were precisely those needed for his first and last name, Dorian Daste. It was as if he was preparing himself by making these sounds, for one day to pronounce his name. Later, he asked me to change the sound of the melody on the piano by taking my hand in an attempt to find variations saying, "Sound" then, "The sound" and, "Changing the sound". I improvised associations with 'Sound, singing sound, changing the sound, finding sounds, singing and dancing' ('sons', 'chanson', 'le son', 'sur le pont d'Avignon'...).

Variations and interiorisation

Dorian delighted in this, but seemed overwhelmed by new emotions with all these words. He tried to find himself again by babbling, "a-eu, a-eu" and bit his hand. He put words to his state of being overwhelmed saying, "oh-la-la, ah la la!", and it appeased him. He said, "Sound, music, changing the sound, new music". Then he put his hands over his ears, closed his eyes and explored very internalized sounds that he made vibrate only for himself, "She, sounds, o, rr, a aommm". He pronounced these sounds from within with delight, in a moment of internalization of what he had gained, by means of sounds he appropriated.

I focused on the "aommmmm" sound that made me think of an oriental sound, very internalized, repeated many times in religious practices in the East. This internalized sound makes the whole body vibrate starting with the 'a' open to the external world followed by the 'o', more interiorized, uttered in the centre of the mouth and prolonged by the 'mmmm'. I told him this, and he responded saying, "Marie-Laure", a name that has the same letters as 'a-o-mmm'. Marie-Odile is a young autistic girl that I have also been seeing for some years.

We were amazed by this session. I told him that it was great to exchange with him, to which he responded by a gesture with his thumb that means great. I named this and imitated him in his gesture. This enabled him to make the gesture a second time while looking at his hand, thus becoming aware of his movement. It seemed to me that this was the first time this had happened. He rejoiced. I had the feeling that a consensus between the tactile and the visual was becoming possible.

The meeting of the senses, which Meltzer (1975) has named consensuality, resonates with the building of a network of syllables, sounds and words in language; a condition for reaching the pleasure of shared communication. While Dorian still used only a small range of words, he seemed to know many more. Nevertheless, he entered into verbal language with pleasure through playing with the variations of sounds, syllables and words that he employed in different modes, like games about spontaneous and improvised meetings.

The mediation of these exchanges, at first at the very archaic level of vibrations, of low sounds and of alternating movements, enabled him to have experiences of shared delight without being overwhelmed in an avalanche of sensorial information that would have been too complex, while consensuality was still not possible.

Responding to unpleasant external sounds by 'sounds from within', gave him the experience of initially sheltering himself from the risk of acoustic invasion. After that, he could build a protective shield capable of filtering what did not suit him, in order to maintain balance and the possibility for outside and inside to meet in a way other than by a radical split. His method of appeasement by releasing himself with screams, by hitting himself and by self-mutilation of his hands, changed gradually into something softer. This happened from the moment a dialogue became possible between the opposite modes of soft and solid, inside and outside, left and right, between him and his environment, by a look accompanied by smiles, and by a verbal dialogue that organized itself spontaneously between words and babbling.

Working on rebuilding his body image helped Dorian to feel more involved with himself and others. At first this was only possible in the setting of individual therapy, where the unpredictability of his environment was reduced. It is gradually becoming possible in the context of his group where he has started to talk more and more often.

Differentiation and shared autonomy

Dorian's shouting, his blows, his self-harm and his psychic 'scatteredness', had been replaced little by little, with a capacity to relate to people and to use language, on the condition that he was assured of each person being properly differentiated, thus avoiding all risk of invasion.

During a musical improvisation in the context of the session, we went to look for instruments in the cupboard. I gave everyone an instrument and marked the difference between generations, his own and that of the two adults, the psychologist in training and myself, "It is the drum of the grown up lady Johanna, the big piano of Chantal and the bells of a young boy". He reacted with a deep sigh of relief, looking at us attentively and smiling. Then he said, "Young boy", as if he felt reassured by the generational difference in the context of the transference.

Dorian, who could not bear any music in his group yet, asked for it during the sessions. He pushed a button on the small electric piano which started to play a pre-recorded melody in a loop. When I noticed that this overwhelmed him, I offered to turn down the volume and make the melody play more slowly until the tempo suited him. Through this, he had the experience that appeasement is possible without having to resort to a release that is psychologically too costly. I interpreted that he could maybe do the same when there was too much noise that disturbed him. He sighed and yawned in relaxation, settled himself by quietly resting his back and head, and then said, "Tranquil".

I was aware of how much Dorian felt invaded by the environment in his group, where he could filter neither his visual nor acoustic perceptions, nor even his movements. In the transference, I surprised myself one day by invading him with various toys that I put in front of him, until he was saturated. He started to get disorganized in order to fight against this invasion, both physically and psychologically. His head, his hands and his tongue performed chaotic movements attempting to cling in an adhesive manner to the walls, as if to avoid the risk of collapse. He was at the point of resorting to shouts of release together with hitting his jaw.

I named my responsibility in this invasion and in his frenetic fight to come to grips with it. By having thus drawn the negative transference onto me, Dorian quickly calmed down. He gave me a grateful smile as if he had finally been unburdened of a heavy responsibility. I told him that he often believed he was under obligation to take interest in everything I offered him visually or acoustically, and that he was doing this to protect me and not to let me down. I added that all this exhausted him and made him forget that he could select what suited him.

From then on he could choose what pleased him and forget the rest without putting me in danger. Reassured, he looked at me with delight. All three of us practiced choosing a toy that interested us, while I put into words that we did not have to worry about the other toys. Dorian was very happy that he did not have to be concerned about me anymore, as he had been before. I reassured him again by committing to look after myself, alone or with the help of the trainee psychologist, Johanna, with whom I symbolically formed a parental couple in the context of the transference.

He was experiencing enjoyment of the toy that he had chosen. All three of us were playing, alone in the presence of others, capable of filtering the perceptions that came from the environment in terms of the individual interest of each of us, in shared autonomy. He especially enjoyed the exchanges between the adults, and we dramatized them, using exchanges and meetings between toys through language. This seemed to help to reinforce his conceivability and his feeling of existence.

It also happened that during moments where he was busy discovering toys on the desk, we explored other objects and put into words our differences and our pleasure at playing alone quietly.

We enacted meetings between adults using toys as mediation, and I interpreted in the transference that Dorian could finally stop having to entertain or take care of the adults, Chantal and Johanna, as he had done until now, forgetting his own existence. He looked at us deeply and happily and started to play happily in his own corner, like a little child. He did not fail in his attempt to imitate us. We prolonged the game by imitating him as well from a distance, in order to then meet again still through the mediation of the toys, and come and go between being reunited and playing with relative independence. We paid special attention to the intermediate moments and to the moments of change, so that he could feel himself to exist even in moments of discontinuity.

The contacts between the educational team assigned to his group and myself, and the exchanges in the context of the sessions with the trainee who was sitting through the therapy, helped the development in the transference of Dorian's fantasy of a good original scene, one from which he could feel himself to exist more and find his place in space, coming from a good connection between his parents.

Primary depression and emergence of language

Because of this, the educational team have been able to support Dorian during the emergence of language that brought back to the forefront a primary depression from his life as a baby that had not yet been worked through. Dorian spent several weeks in his group crying.

One day I walked past his group when he was crying in that way. He was on the ground, out of his mould and his chair. Kneeling, he was crying because he was unable to get himself up as he wanted. He was crying like a baby in distress, without the notion of asking for help or being comforted. He was alone with himself and his distress. I approached him and said that he felt completely lost, that he was trying to straighten up and was not succeeding, that he was loosing his balance when he would have wanted to be nice and tall. I suggested that he lean on me so as to be able to get his torso into a vertical position. I also said to him, while his project worker looked on attentively, that when he cried it was not always easy to know what was wrong and that perhaps his project worker would better understand if he called her and talked to her. He continued to cry, wanting rather to be recognized in his cries as a baby in distress. I then told him that his project worker had noticed that he was crying, and that we could practice calling her together by whispering, "Benedicte!" Dorian stopped crying and practiced pronouncing the name of his project worker several times, whispering. Benedicte spoke, telling him that she understood much better when he called her using words and congratulated him. If well supported, going through a primary depression offers a renewed possibility for language to emerge, as well as connectedness and communication.

**

To re-contact the power to play on the archaic level, contributes actively to the installation of a communicative and lively language that can be transposed to other contexts, as was the case with Dorian. Our work as therapists is made easier when we remain flexible in using the different registers of our capacity to play, from archaic sensations to secondary thinking.

The work of putting into words the sensoriality achieved in his mouth gave Dorian the opportunity for archaic experiences of the primitive oral zone and has revived the cathexis of a cannibalistic orality in the pleasure of aggression connected with the teeth. A degree of ambivalence could then start to develop, so the opposites are no longer split but in a dialogue, with good integrity of the bodily self. Investing in the mouth is one of the conditions by which a child may feel inclined to talk.

In the light of having followed Dorian, it appears to me essential to make the observation that autistic children who cannot yet bear the voice of others, nor even the rhythmic sounds that one finds in music, fix at former experiences but understand verbal language as soon as the therapist talks to them about what interests them. Their experiences are sometimes at very archaic levels, like that of vibrations or movement. A shared emotion can thus become possible and restores an erased bodily ego. The mouth becomes the terrain of exploration of space, sensations and vibrations, which support the emergence of verbal language in the meeting with the other.

Although in existential beginnings, the formation of sensorial integration follows the chronological stages of development, each of these stages may be questioned at any time, not only from a developmental point of view, but also in a parallel way. We can also be attentive in the course of analysis with neurotic patients, to precocity in certain fixations, to sensorial elements as well as the vibratory composition of the voice.

CHAPTER SIX

The return of the absent father

Jacob Segal

L ast spring, at a discussion group I attended, I heard a metaphor about the relation between play and power, "If you want to hear music on a CD player, you have to press the Power button first, and then the Play button. If you press Play without pressing the Power first, you will get nothing". There is no play without power first!

I associate this metaphor with the psychodynamic forces in the inner world of a child or a baby suffering from father absence, by which I mean the absence of a sufficiently strong, warm and present father, introjected in the child's mind as an unconscious source of inner power. A father who is absent, physically or emotionally, creates a hole or wound in the inner world of the child. I am talking here about the inner preconception of the child of a functioning father that meets frustration and creates thinking, or a bad object, if the child is unable to bear the absence (Bion, 1967b). Moreover, I am also talking about the child's need for a good enough father, an external father who is needed when we deal with ego vulnerability and dependence (Winnicott, 1963).

The integration of this dialectic of the role of inner and outer realities is touching a complicated debate in psychoanalysis (Berman, 2004).

In the therapeutic setting I am working in, the therapist and patient create together, intermediate space or play space (Herzog, 2001) that moves between inner and outer realities, according to the state of being of the patient or the phase of therapy. Phillips (1988) writes, "Transitional space breaks down when either inner or outer reality begins to dominate the scene, just as conversation stops if one of the participants takes over".

I would like to return to the inner wound created by the absence of the real father and also by the inner processes happening within the child who has an introjection of an absent father. This wound will constitute a threat to the child's sense of security, and may produce a preoccupation with issues of power and vulnerability. In this way, the experience of father absence may damage part of the child's capacity for playfulness with life, with himself and his objects.

The absent father, by my definition, is the external father who is nonexistent, non-functioning or insignificant. It is also the image of the father internalized in the inner world of mother, child and father, which constitutes a central, powerful part of the inner world, consciously and unconsciously affecting one's inner and external life. The concept of absent father as I use it, is related to the absent father image and the father's missing functions which the patient brings to the playground of the transference relations as an unconscious cause of his psychic pain and deep anxieties.

Developmentally, the task of endorsing the child's play is performed by both parents, each with a somewhat characteristic mode of play interaction (Herzog, 2001). In the transference—countertransference relations of an absent father patient, there is always an enactment of the missed play with father, with all its complexities and the personal colours of the patient's projections and introjections.

According to Winnicott (1952), "There is no such thing as a baby", meaning that a baby would neither live nor develop without its mother. Green (1977) said that, "There is no such thing as a mother and baby" alluding to the presence of the father figure in the mother's unconscious emotional world. Etchegoyen (2002) added, in the book *The Importance of Fathers*, "There is no such thing as a father, without the mother's relationship with the father". It seems to me that one of the missing sentences within the complex object relations of the father-mother-child triangle is, "There is no baby without a father figure, often a real father, and in any case a father in the child's inner world".

Etchegoyen (2002) says that it is still uncertain today how the father contributes to, and affects his children's development. She raises two important questions:

1. Are fathers really necessary?
2. Are fathers different from mothers?

I add another question to this discussion:

3. Is the absence of a father different from the absence of a mother?

Freud (1923) plays with the question of the importance and powerful influence of the father on his children:

> "Behind the ego ideal there lies hidden the first and most important identification of all, the identification with the father, which takes place in the prehistory of every person. This is apparently not in the first instance the consequence or outcome of an object-cathexis; it is a direct and immediate identification and takes place earlier than any object-cathexis". (pp. 39–40)

But then in a footnote to this paragraph Freud notes:

> "Perhaps it would be safer to say, "Identification with the parents" for before a child had arrived at definite knowledge of the difference between the sexes, the lack of a penis, it does not distinguish in value between its father and its mother".

What then, is the truth according to Freud? Is he playing with the reader in order to raise the important question that Etchegoyen (2002) raised: "Are fathers different from mothers?"

Freud brings forward two points of view, firstly, that there is a difference between identifications with father and mother, in that the influence of the father on certain parts of the psyche is more powerful than that of the mother, and secondly, that in infancy there are no differences between father and mother in the child's identifications. Elsewhere, Freud (1930) related to the baby's helplessness and his need for his father, "I cannot think of any need in childhood as strong as the need for the father's protection".

From my experience of working with adults and children, I believe that every boy and girl has a strong need for his or her father in two important ways:

1. An inborn constitutional need for emotional contact with the biological father. By emotional contact I mean the child's feelings and fantasies about the biological father, including a need for a real relationship with the biological father; *Paternal attachment*.
2. A need for a present and functioning father figure who contributes to the child's psychic development. This father figure can be a male figure from outer reality (grandfather, uncle, stepfather etc.) or an inner father in the mother's internal world; *Paternal functions*.

Such terms as "absent father" (Burgner, 1986; Lewis, 1991; Gill, 1991; Kirschner, 1992; Mancia, 1993), "dead father" (McDougall, 1989), "the lost father" (Green, 2009) and "father hunger" (Herzog, 2001), are attempts by psychoanalysis to conceptualize the deep and powerful emotional effects of different types of deprivation in the dyadic or triangular relationship with the father, and the emotional wound such deprivations leave in a person's soul.

Mancia (1993) describes, from clinical work with perversion, many cases in which the parallel of an absent father is a symbiotic, fused mother. In such cases, claims Mancia, the father is absent not just physically but also psychologically, since he is vague and distant, unable to understand the child's pragmatic needs. Such a father cannot become the child's real identification model.

Lewis (1991) claims there are many reasons for a father's constant absence along a child's development and that such absence could affect the developing child in various ways. On the other hand, he says, the absence of a father does not necessarily cause psychopathology and is not in itself, reason for psychotherapeutic intervention.

In my opinion, actual absence of a father, even if it does not cause obvious pathology, always creates an unconscious emotional absence or wound in the child or adult suffering from this that brings about a compulsive repetition of situations illustrating the absence of a father and the need for his return to the conscious inner world of experience.

One of the changes in psychoanalysis after Freud was the understanding that the first three years of life are not solely about a dyadic relationship between mother and baby, father and baby, or father and mother. Melanie Klein and her followers describe a triangular relationship and an early Oedipus complex taking place already in the first year of life.

The "primal scene" was first described by Freud (1918) in the case of the "wolf man". The primal scene fantasy is described by Freud as an archaic heritage of innate ideas which cause every baby to create some kind of fantasy of parental intercourse which is conflated by the developing child's real and imagined experience.

Britton (1989) described Klein's use of the "primal scene" fantasy as a focus of what she called the oedipal situation. I now illustrate the enactment of the primal scene fantasy in a session of dyadic play therapy with a mother and child who had an absent father.

Case 1: "The mother's tail"

A single mother and her 4-year-old son came to my clinic about a year ago. As soon as they walked in, it seemed as if this was a dyadic therapy, in the sense that mother and child were attached to one another.

Several months later I named the way they continued entering the room "the mother's tail". The mother walks in, and the child is attached behind, almost invisible to me.

The mother's name is Ronit, the child's name, Roni. The mother reports that her wish for a child was the only reason for her relationship with the father. They separated while she was pregnant, and in fact Roni never saw his father, who died of a terminal illness when the child was two.

During the first sessions, Roni constantly lay down on the mother, putting his head near her vagina as if wanting to return to the womb. His mother described him as a child with sensory sensitivity, developmental difficulties and tantrums, culminating in the child banging his head against the bed as a baby, while she is terrified and helpless in the face of the tantrum.

After intense work in dyadic and individual sessions with the mother over several months, significant changes occurred in their lives. The mother intensified her relationship with a boyfriend she had been seeing, and began going out with him in the evenings, which she had not allowed herself to do before.

The mother described Roni as being able to swim with a flotation ring for the first time without her holding him. Sometimes in the playroom, Roni separated from the mother's body and during some sessions, played with me while the mother was sitting aside reading a book. My countertransference was that I did not quite exist for Roni. When I asked him a direct question, he did not answer. Sometimes he whispered the answer in his mother's ear, and she repeated what he had said. Usually, even when he played with me, he did not address me directly.

Roni arrived restless and jittery to one of our sessions. When I asked what had happened, the mother said they had a fight in the car on the way to the session. The radio was playing trance music which she does not like but which he wanted left on. The mother refused and he had a tantrum, "Like he often had when he was a baby."

For the first time, I witnessed live in the therapy room, the babyhood tantrums the mother had described earlier in therapy. Roni clung to his mother and hurt her. Mother said, "Leave me alone, I don't like this hug". Roni did not relent, hanging on to his mother like a baby, making babyish, howl-like sounds. The mother asked if he wanted a hug and he responded with angry baby sounds, pulled her hand, hung onto her and seemed as if about to tear her blouse. Ronit protested with growing anger. Eventually she said, "I won't have it, you can't do whatever you like to my body. I'm moving to the chair". Now Ronit was on the chair and Roni and I on the carpet. I sat and tried to address Roni, but he responded to all my suggestions with angry voices.

Roni lay on the carpet, covering his face with his hands. His mother's attempts to address him were also answered with angry baby sounds. I tried to talk to Ronit and let Roni calm down. However, whenever his mother and I tried to talk, he made stronger angry noises. When we tried to ignore those, Roni went into a tantrum, hit the games in the boxes near him, throwing them all over the room while lying on the floor with his head in his hands. At this point I was thinking that in the schizo-paranoid state Roni was in during that session, any connection between his mother and me was experienced in transference as a re-enactment of a violent, aggressive primal scene, so that at that moment, the talk between Ronit and myself was unbearable for him thus attacked by him in all possible ways.

I interpreted for Roni, "It's so scary and annoying for you when mother and I are together and you're excluded. In the situation you're in right now, it's unbearable for you". Roni calmed down somewhat after this interpretation, and silence fell. I drove a toy car towards his hand. First he resisted, but suddenly he got up and we played quietly with the cars crashing into each other and the wall. He slowly seemed to relax and even laugh delightedly when he succeeded in getting one car to touch another car or the wall. Mother and child left the session holding hands, and it seemed the intensive tension they had arrived with had calmed.

Britton (1992) asks, "Will our love survive knowledge, particularly our growing awareness of the separateness of our love objects and their relationships with others that exclude us (p. 45)?" Stated in other words, will the growing baby be able to deal with the emotional reality of the depressive position and the pain of the oedipal situation?

In moving from the different, complementary dyads with mother and father to a triangular space, the baby begins to see a pair of parents who have a relationship. The baby's ability to bear the oedipal pain of the realization that he is not his mother's sole, exclusive source of pleasure, and that he is excluded from the parental bedroom, the ability to be in a position to view his parents' relationship from which he's excluded, depends on whether he had a good-enough dyad previously. It is very difficult for the baby to surrender the totality of the dyadic relationship; paradise. Yet it is this surrender which creates a space for the child to see and be seen, to view his parents' relationship without destroying or being destroyed.

Herzog (2001) conceptualizes play in child analysis and adult analysis as the action language of doing, redoing and undoing. He describes play as a mode for representing, communicating and trying on, both within the evolving self system and between the self and others. This second case is of a woman patient with an absent father who projected into the therapy space, the powerful influence of her father's absence on her self and object relations reflected in the transference—countertransference, as well as her actions and verbal associations.

Case 2: The deserting absent father

Tami was 35, married with three children, a senior high-tech employee. She turned to therapy after incidents of fainting during stress. Her parents divorced when she was 10 years old, and her father moved to a distant country. She lived with her mother and sisters. Towards the end of high school, a yearbook was produced and each student was asked to give things which characterize him or her. Tami said to me, "I felt there was nothing special about me. I was a good student, fairly popular, but there was nothing outstanding I could say about myself. Actually the only thing that made me special was the fact my father had deserted us, which I couldn't write in a yearbook".

Within the transference-countertransference, I felt from the start a sense of desperate neediness from Tami for my assistance and closeness. In time, Tami described therapy as the most significant thing in her life, and occasionally thanked me for the care and steadiness in the relationship with me.

After two years of therapy, there arose one day when I had to cancel all therapy sessions for personal reasons. When I called the patients scheduled for that day, I simply forgot to call Tami whose session was the first, early morning session. Tami called me after waiting for several minutes outside the clinic. I apologized and made a free, alternative appointment. In discussing the incident, Tami responded indifferently. She said people sometimes forget appointments and she saw no reason to make a fuss. She did not turn up for the next session, without notification, and when I called to ask what had happened, she said she seemed to think she wanted to have a break in therapy. I invited her to a session to discuss this. At the meeting I told Tami it seemed to me that if we did not discuss what had happened, the therapy would never come back to life. To my surprise, she did not resist the interpretation and said she was pleased I saw how fragile the situation was for her. I shared with her the fact that the forgetting that had happened was very untypical of me and that, in my opinion, although I took full responsibility and sincerely apologized for hurting her, I assumed this had happened unconsciously because of something re-enacted between us that was connected to her father's desertion, some sort of opportunity as an adult woman to work through the anxieties, hurt and anger over the father's desertion. Tami remained silent for a long time and then, in a shaky voice, crying silently, said, "It really wasn't terrible. I just felt again that familiar feeling that

I was worthless, nothing, air. Why should you even think of me or remember me?"

Tami described herself standing in front of the door feeling like a helpless, paralysed child. "I wanted to just go and never return. But I thought, you're an adult woman, maybe something happened to him? So I called you. On the one hand, I could hear your surprise, so I do believe you didn't do it deliberately. On the other hand, maybe I'd have preferred you to have acted deliberately than to forget me! The insult came later, with anger, and I just wanted never to see you again. The feeling does remind me of my father. I've been thinking of him for years. If he could leave me and remain far away all those years, I must be nothing for him. In my adolescence he contacted me, invited me to the country he was living in. I told him I wasn't interested in seeing him and couldn't believe he dared invite me as if nothing had happened. He cared only about himself and his money, and didn't care about us, so why should I care about him? He was a stranger. All my life since I was ten, I could count on the fingers of one hand the times I saw him; he's no part of my life."

After we had worked through the crisis of the missed session intensively, Tami brought a dream. "I'm sitting with mother and my sisters eating and suddenly father comes home and then I understand in my dream that I had invited him to eat with us. I get up and invite father to enter and join the meal." Tami cries and says, "I never dreamed about my father, certainly nothing good like this. In reality I don't think I'd have invited him, because I'm mostly angry with him or ignore him, I feel he doesn't deserve it."

I interpret Tami's willingness for the first time since therapy beginning, to let her father enter therapy at her invitation. Tami responds with a stream of memories from the time before her father left. Father took her for a whole day, just the two of them, to an amusement park; she and her father setting up a chimney in the living room; Father lying in bed on a Saturday and she jumping on him while laughing and playing. The relationship with her father, mourning his leaving, and the latent deep wish for a mutual, good relationship with him become the therapy's central theme, including changes in herself, her life with her husband and children and thoughts about renewing contact with her father, but this time at her initiative.

Freud (1908) in the preface to *"The interpretation of dreams"* says:

"This book was a portion of my self analysis, my reaction to my father's death—that is to say, to the most important event, the most poignant loss, of a man's life. Having discovered that this was so, I felt unable to obliterate the traces of the experience".

The third case material presents an adult male patient who lost his father as a boy and is still struggling with the consequence of this tragic death as an adult both in life, and in a psychoanalytic psychotherapy.

Case 3: "Swamp of death"

At his first meeting, Tal said that when he was 14 years old his father died suddenly of heart failure. The father had been on a business trip and died in a hotel overseas. Tal said he remembered little of that period around his father's death but he thought he had "drawn an iron curtain" and continued with his life. The way he talked about his father, as well as his attitude to me in the transference, were characterized by aloofness and rationality. Tal noted his father is a stranger to him, he feels distanced from him and he does not exist for him.

After three years in therapy, Tal brought a dream which he termed "the swamp of death". "He's a pilot crashing with his plane into a swamp. Then he tries walking in the swamp and failing. Ahead he sees a huge man-sized grasshopper. The grasshopper has huge bulging eyes that attract Tal to look at them but when he does, he sees something blocked, dead and sad. He sees there are many grasshopper carcasses under water and is scared and disgusted to walk on in case he steps on them and their limbs break. It's a swamp of death, full of dead bodies". In association to the dream Tal said, "This grasshopper's eyes are like my father's". It reminded him of a fantasy he had of seeing a door to the dead world when a skeleton walks out who is his father. When he comes closer and wants to talk or hug him, someone arrives saying the skeleton must return to the world of the dead and they disappear behind the door.

Tal asked me, "What do you feel when you meet me, when I arrive for a session?" When I asked what he thinks, he replied, "You seem embarrassed and I'm embarrassed too". He said he perceived me from early on in therapy as distanced and restrained. When I asked what he would like, Tal was silent then said, "I'd like us to be closer. I'd like you to ask how I am, not out of duty but to ask how I feel. I'd like more warmth between us. I'd like to be able to consult with you and trust you". I said, "What you're saying is that now you're finding it hard to trust me, to consult with me, and you feel a certain distance and difficulty to get emotionally closer". Tal replied, "Yes, I realize I have a part in this too".

Later in the session, Tal said that the return of his father might be difficult for him. On the one hand he feels unbearable longing, that he cannot go on living without the presence, hug and advice from father, but on the other hand it might cause him to drown in a sea of pain, depression and anger as he feels the "bad father" had hurt him.

Tal describes the "great power"; the power of emotional detachment. This way he will not be hurt, would not drown in the swamp of sorrow and would not become dependent on me and therapy. Distance and recoiling from dependence on the one hand, while yearning for a close relationship on the other hand, are the central characteristics of transference.

Conclusion

The clinical cases which have been presented were chosen as different illustrations of the typical play that takes place between the therapist and the child or adult patient suffering from father absence.

Lewis (1991) claims that growing up with an absent father causes problems in transference, since the ability to reconstruct the relationship with a father figure in therapy is missing. In other words, the deficiencies in the internal object relationship, because of a lack of external relationship with a live and close father figure, creates difficulties in relating intimately with a masculine-paternal figure. In my experience with patients without fathers, the influence of the father absence on the patient-therapist relationships is powerful.

There is a short story by Henry (1904); "A Strange Story". It is about a father who went out one evening to get some medicine for his 5-year-old sick daughter. He never came back ... The little girl recovered and grew up. As a woman she married and also had a little 5-year-old girl. One night, by a remarkable coincidence, her girl became sick on the anniversary of the disappearance of the woman's father. Her worried husband wanted to go downtown and get some medicine. The woman cried, "No, you will not go [...] You, too, might disappear forever, and then forget to come back". Suddenly the door opened, and an old man entered the room. "Hello, here is grandpa", said the little girl, who had recognized him before any of the others did. The old man drew a bottle of medicine from his pocket and gave the girl a spoonful. She got well immediately.

This short story shows symbolically, the psychic wound present in a child whose father is absent. But it can also be used as a symbol for the possibility of the return of the absent father. Sometimes, after many years in the therapeutic playground, such a return from the unconsciousness of the missing father occurs in the transference/ countertransference and through the dreams and associations of the patient. This return has a powerful healing effect on the patient's inner life.

The therapeutic interaction in such cases is often characterized by two types of transference/countertransference that involve typical emotions, defences and object relationships.

I would call the first type *detached father transference*, corresponding with Lewis' (1991) definition and characterized by a distant relationship with the therapist, a correct and detached relationship, resistance to talk about the therapist/patient relationship as the arena of significant occurrences, sometimes devaluation and contempt of the therapist, and attacks on the therapeutic setting. The emotional atmosphere is distant and cool with rare events of crisis and powerful emotional outbursts.

The child I described, Roni, behaved towards me in most of the sessions as if I were air, and talked to me only via whispering in his mother's ear. However, in the session I described, he had a rare temper tantrum and attacked the toys in the playroom as an expression of the difficulty to witness, from a schizoparanoid point of view, the verbal interaction between the mother and therapist.

Tal also established, for a significant part of the therapy, a distant, correct relationship. The therapist's sense in the countertransference is of a non-existent entity, functional, technical or insignificant. This feeling in countertransference is often accompanied by a sense of boredom and sometimes separation or desertion anxiety.

The second type could be termed *father hunger transference* after Herzog's (2001) term "father hunger", described as a strong, persistent emotional situation of yearning for a father, found among children who lost their father following divorce. Transference relationships of "father hunger" are characterized by a strong need for the therapist, who is perceived as a powerful figure with strong influence on the patient's emotional situation. This strong relationship presents itself during the first sessions, sometimes at surprisingly powerful speed.

The patient tries to appease the therapist and concur with him, from a place of great neediness, deprivation and desertion anxiety. The parallel in countertransference could be feelings of a saviour accompanied by "rescue fantasies" and sometimes an unconscious wish to replace the absent father and become the ideal father whom the patient longs for. When there is empathic failure or injury by the therapist upon the patient's expectations of an ideal object, the patient might react by leaving therapy, or by feelings of terrible hurt and anger towards the therapist who has ruined his chance to finally get the beneficial father yearned for all those years. When the patient has let himself feel the need for a father, the frustration of this need in the transference/countertransference is experienced as a catastrophe, and often the disappointment with the therapist is irreversible. Tami's therapy described here was characterized by such a process. The enactment of the desertion of the father in the transference/countertransference and the capacity to play with it, enabled working through and reconstruction of the father's desertion and later a change in her object relations with a more integrative father figure, resulting in a real change in her relationships with male figures outside the therapy.

The therapist must be able to survive crises and anxieties aroused in transference/countertransference and make it playful in order to help the patient make the unconscious touching of the psychic wound of the absent father an opportunity for reparation and creative growth.

Such creative play with the powerful, inner, absent father, projected into the clinical space, enables patient and therapist to experience object relationships connected with the absent father that have closeness and contact, frustration and corresponding disappointment. This then raises the possibility for reparation and working through the powerful repressed emotions concerning the departure of the absent father and his return in the therapeutic playground.

In *The Invention of Solitude* (1982), American author Paul Auster describes his father, "He had no wife, no family that depended on him, no one whose life would be altered by his absence ... Eventually, it would be as though he had never lived at all. Even before his death he had been absent, and long ago the people closest to him had learned to accept this absence, to treat it as the fundamental quality of his being. Now that he was gone, it would not be difficult for the world to absorb the fact that he was gone forever ... If, while he was alive, I kept looking for him, kept trying to find the father who was not there, now that he is dead I still feel as though I must go on looking for him. Death has not changed anything".

In such cases, the patient comes to therapy in order to seek his absent inner father.

The therapist's ability to recognize the absence and enable the therapeutic journey of meeting in the transference relationship with the absent father, will enable processes of mourning and reconnecting with the father within the patient's inner world. This renewed meeting, which could be termed *the return of the absent father*, sometimes occurs as a repetition through the transference/countertransference playground, or through the reconstruction of the past through the patient's associations, dreams and memories and the therapist's interpretations of them. It should be noted that there is also a creation of something entirely new that is aroused by the analytic situation (Freud, 1937; Green, 2000) which enables a new and powerful emotional reunion of the daughter or son with the father, sometimes after years of distance and separation. Such a reunion will enable a significant change in the inner world and emotional life of the patient.

CHAPTER SEVEN

Power and play: A tale of denigration and idealisation

Gerhard Wilke

Introduction

To begin with, a question: what might the link be between the two apparently opposing and complementary forces of power and play? Power conjures up abusive adults while play invokes thoughts of innocent and playful children. In my musings on this theme it also struck me that we psychotherapists, as a community, have a propensity to idealise play and denigrate power. This tendency gives us an inauthentic sense of authority when we are outside the sacred space of the therapy room. We prefer to be helpless helpers, rather than powerful movers and shakers. Noble and passive victims are our preferred playmates! It has become necessary to reflect on what makes us afraid in the face of external power, attracts us to being at the mercy of fate in the shape of the modernisers of our Health Systems, and prevents us from shaping our own destiny. It is high time that we looked at how we can recover a sense of play as professional therapists. Through this "as if" quality of play, I think we can re-learn to hold power, meet "money givers" as equals and have the patience to survive as an established form of treatment.

Link between power and play

To start in a conventional way, I think it prudent for psychotherapists to look at Winnicott's view of the link between power and
play (Winnicott, 1971). In a good enough environment, aggression,
the power to destroy, defend and oppress, gets integrated into the
self and can be sublimated into work, creation, culture and play.
In an undependable and depriving environment, aggression ends
up being dissociated, projected outwards and acted out. The self
is not able to be held by the other in a relationship but tests the
holding authority figure through hate and boundary testing. In
regressive and traumatised states therefore, our capacity to play
and symbolise in a potential space between me and not me gets
lost and replaced by concrete thinking. A defence which signifies a
"false self" tries to cope with a failing environment which is projec-
tively filled with the overwhelming power of fate and undependable authority figures. The false self is unconscious of its desire to
re-connect with an accepting parental figure; it is desperate to learn
for the first time or re-learn the art of presenting a true self, through
the playful use of the object in a good enough relationship (Phillips,
1988). Perhaps that is the current position of our profession within
the Health System. We, as a community, feel the loss of a nurturing
welfare state mother, and need to hold ourselves together, with the
help of a false self, until we have recovered our true professional
self-confidence. Only with a good enough sense of professional
worth can we engage in a power-play with our therapeutic rivals
and the reformed and modernised Health System. As long as we
feel like step-children lumbered with step-parents, we will be liable to think and act concretely in the presence of others; especially
those whom we think have power over us.

For Winnicott, playing allows the child and the adult to explore
the otherness of reality in interaction with a caregiver or a holding
environment. We ideally need the relationship between therapist
and patient, health employee and Health Manager to be a playful,
developmental space. I suspect that the current experience of psychotherapists with the Health System is depriving and restricting
rather than enabling. In Winnicott's terms, we are collectively in
the position of the patient who has no capacity for play and cannot yet make use of a care giver who wants to open a potential

space in which therapy or work can be conceptualised as play, an act of creation rather than compliance (Winnicott, 1965). In such a situation, the capacity to play has first to be re-learned before real work and analysis can begin. We, as a profession, are in this situation. We need to explore whether we can use our therapeutic skills beyond the clinical setting in meetings with those who hold us to account. The aim would be to restore the environmental conditions in the presence of our organisational "parents" for play power to replace the prevalent mood of powerlessness. When it is necessary, we need to give ourselves permission to turn the power relationship upside down and take charge of a situation because we have the skills and insight to move things on by embodying an authority figure.

Forces of fate or destiny

Let me now ask, how might we recover, as individuals and as a community, from being at the mercy of forces seemingly beyond our control? The transition from victimhood to self-determination within a constraining context is, for Christopher Bollas in his book Forces of Destiny, at the heart of every journey through life (Bollas, 1991). The reform of all state health systems has put professionals in the position of having to adapt their inner self-ideal to a changed outside world. All our Health Systems have, since the Thatcher— Reagan—Gorbachev revolution, turned from being a nurturing mother into a persecuting father under the guise of accountability, evidence based practice, transparency and choice for politicians and patients. It is not surprising that we feel overwhelmed and persecuted. The trouble is that giving in to the feelings of persecution lands us in the paranoid-schizoid position and we lose our capacity to think analytically.

Bollas (1991) suggests that we all have the power to make a choice between two opposing but connected forces: first, that of being the object of fate, a force that is out there and overpowering, without apparent connection to our own lives; second, that we accept that our destiny is defined by the particular family, society and age into which we are placed. We turn ourselves into victims of fate if we resent the essential unfairness of our birth. Alternatively, we can begin to shape our destiny, within limits, if we make the best of the situation. It is by accepting that we have choices within limits, not absolute free will or power as Nietzsche might have wished, that we can recover a sense of being in charge of our lives and professional situation (Russel, 2000). This self-reassertion, in the face of harsh reality, is as precarious as the ego's attempt to survive the demands of the id and the super-ego. The ego, just like each of us in our professional role, is always struggling to maintain a sense of integration while holding on to the capacity to think, relate and play.

The Health Systems of Western Europe were, until the Neo-liberal modernisation drive, good and care giving potential spaces, worthy of Winnicott's (1965) gentle language. Now they have become spaces filled with the fear of death and fragmentation. Our professional world is an experience associated with the symptoms of Post Traumatic Stress Disorder. We can try to acknowledge this state, mourn our loss and own how we have colluded in giving birth to the conservative counter-revolution. The conservative drive to bring the public sector under control and stem cost expansion followed on from the 60s revolt and the expansion of the welfare state. The power we, as psychotherapists, gained through the rapid expansion of services, made us liable to become omnipotent. We began to ignore the competition and scorned critical research, which could have bolstered our professional recognition. Instead, we deluded ourselves that we were superior to the bean-counters.

Well, the bean counters are back and confirm the theory of Elias on power. He argued that power is not located in any one person but emerges between people in a relationship or between groups in a social context (Elias & Scotson, 1993). Elias's work rests on Freud who, in Mass Psychology and Ego Development, clearly illustrated that the power of the charismatic leader depends on the projective wishes of the merged followers, and that the fusion of the mass flows from the willingness of the leader to submit to the wishes of the group, usually by fuelling the denigration of an enemy (Freud, 1921). Leader and followers are nothing without the existence of the excluded or marginalised other. The history of psychoanalysis gave us an inheritance of fearing other therapies, ignoring other treatment approaches and quarrelling amongst ourselves. The time for self-absorbed play is over; the time for power play has overtaken us. We are charged to co-operate and play as a group against an organised opposition and we will play more successfully, if we adopt an analytic view of power, which places the powerful and powerless in a relationship that is simultaneously symmetrical and asymmetrical.

Location of power in the space between

So, instead of talking about states of power, powerlessness and empowerment, I suggest we start thinking in terms of power being an ordinary and normal ingredient of all social relationships, and that the amount of power held varies between the parties involved as there are no social relationships without status differentials. The fewer status differences there are the more psychic energy goes into maintaining the narcissism of little difference. In other words, flat teams and an innocent world of equal beings without a bad side, held by those of us who believe in hierarchy free multi-disciplinary teams, is a delusional belief system. What Elias shows in his work is that power is best thought of as a balance of power and a differential rate of power distribution. With such a picture of power, we get a sense of changing power relations over time and in a social space, imperceptible to those involved. We got used to being powerful as a profession between 1950 and 1980 and since then we have a sense of losing our power and becoming marginalised. When we felt powerful, others had the feelings we now have. Those who used to feel oppressed by our power, behavioural therapists and straight psychiatrists, are now in the ascendancy, and feel that the gods are smiling on them.

But, as I said, power relations are dynamic and never static in a non-totalitarian system. They can be of a playful nature, terrorising, or something more complex in-between. What determines the difference is the nature of the interaction, just as in therapy. Part of the dynamic of power relations is the propensity of the powerful to use minority groups to define the boundary between insiders and outsiders. This theory allows us to go on thinking therapeutically whilst looking at society and how it changes in a relational way. The minority is never without power, it might feel crushed but it still has an influence on how things will pan out in the future, irrespective of whether those involved are conscious or unconscious of this process. What is certain, Elias argues, is that the power-dynamic between insiders and outsiders reverses over time and as the ex-outsiders tend to repeat the behaviour patterns of the ex-insiders, when they get to be in power, each victory is transitory and sets up the next cycle of rise and fall (Elias, 1991).

The current modernisers and evidence based power brokers, mirror the Puritans during the Protestant Reformation or the Inquisition during the Catholic Counter-Reformation who thought that all humans, but especially professionals, cannot be trusted to keep their own house in order. In part, the modernisers have come to see the world this way because we, their objects of improvement, actually did fail to deal with the abusers amongst us out of a misguided sense of libertarianism. As such, many among us became omnipotent about our power to cure everyone and everything. Such claims always invite ridicule. Just as traditional medicine and natural science based psychology, which are in the power position at present, overestimate the importance of the body and the brain, we persist in giving too much power to the unconscious and unconscious forces. The split between the body and the mind, and professional communities associated with this division is at the heart of the power struggle within the current Health Systems. An 'us and them' struggle is in progress between those who embrace a practice of psychological therapy based on organically traceable causes, and those who believe in the power of unconscious defences in response to environmental failure. The losers in this ideological battle are liable to be excluded from the list of preferred forms of treatment offered with the help of state subsidies. What policy makers do not seem to want to contemplate or play with is the idea that it is not an either—or but an as well as situation.

Let me therefore ask, what lays behind the wish to reduce psychological treatment to a simplistic formula of either it does or does not work, or, it is or is not cost-effective? In my book on the Health reforms in the UK, *How to be a Good Enough GP*, I put forward the idea that we work in a "Keep Death at Bay" system (Wilke, 2001). The taboo in the current political dialogue is that a lot of services are not geared to healing but to humane and chronic management of patients. I suspect psychotherapy's future lies in this taboo segment of the Health System. Until this extremely significant work gets valued and is restored as a core task for therapists and health managers, we are going to struggle to compete with other treatment modalities that promise easy gains and measurable improvements. As a group analyst, I feel that we have unconsciously been delegated the task of holding on to the meaning of "decent treatment" of those who are marginal to completely rationalised and commercialised society. We have to become fully conscious of this in order to recover our position as players with power in the Psychiatric field. The population is ageing, politicians are denying the consequences and the demand for treatment for chronic sufferers is increasing. We are best equipped to meet this demand and play around with it, saying that we are able to cover the market segment for people who need care rather than a cure. In Britain, at least there is evidence that the "internal market" of the Health System is beginning to assign the market segment of Personality Disorders to psychoanalytically based treatment methods. We are being, either by design or default, turned into the experts most able to work with those patients "who no-one else" wants to treat anymore. The trap in this niche market is that marginal patients get marginalised therapists, but I suspect this picture varies enormously throughout Europe.

Winnicott (1971) formulated a powerful vision of hope and development associated with play and transitional phenomena while denying the role of the father and the traumatising power of radical social change. Like the current managers, he avoided dwelling on the pain and loss involved in coping with making transitions. Winnicott underestimated our need to defend against loss and the attraction of engaging with others, in a potential space, through resistance and aggression. The potential spaces Winnicott so lovingly invited us to work in, do not just confront us with the potential for growth and authentic self-expression but also make us liable to fetishise the power of others and the helplessness of ourselves (Davis & Wallbridge, 1983). As long as we give others all the power and cast ourselves in the role of the object of fate, we will also have a valence to "volunteer" on society's behalf to function as a "social toilet" for its psychological waste, whilst others play the game of grabbing the available resources of the state to "return the stragglers to work".

Socially unconscious delegation processes

Thinking about what is happening in terms of the social unconscious, I would argue that society delegates the task of working through "unwanted" psychic material to certain sub-groups.

This can be observed between generations in traumatised families where the children of the survivors of persecution and disaster take over the task of dealing with the guilt associated with being alive. Social order within society is maintained by punishing deviants and, thereby, reinforcing normal behaviour. We all use politicians to deal with making society work and serve as potential scapegoats when it fails. Politicians, as guardians of social integration, unconsciously delegate their concerns about death, insanity and lack of control to certain institutions and professional groups. Psychiatry, Social Work, Residential Care and Psychotherapy can be seen in this way. No wonder members of these institutions feel powerless rather than powerful. The existence of these containers of deviance and madness, allows the rest of society to have a sense of normality.

What I am suggesting is that we, as a profession, embody the boundary between established insiders and marginalised outsiders. It is reasonable to ask what makes us liable to "unconsciously" volunteer for such a role, and what is the need of another group to export such existential fears? There is a pathological and a healthy reason for this dynamic. The Health Reforms are part of a drive to "normalise" the professionals so that they stop being privileged beings with power over patients. Politicians want professionals to become ordinary cost and profit centres, subject to control and accountability. The relentless drive is to prefer treatment methods that are perceived as cheap, cost effective and can be measured and evidenced. We are outsiders on all these counts as analytic therapists; we need time, we want space and cannot predict outcomes. Logically, we are therefore ideally situated to serve as the containers for the split off vulnerable parts of all those sub-groups in the Health System who promise to comply with the requirements of an accountancy lead organisation.

What we collectively contribute to this scenario is our insistence on splitting the world into bad managers and good clinicians. We tend to flee from the profane and public interactions with management, into the sacred and private encounter with patients. This kind of splitting is understandable and partly healthy but it is also a refusal to accept that elections and global processes of change have overtaken us. From my perspective, we must resist the split into sacred clinical work and profane political engagement. I would urge you, individually and collectively, to open the boundary between the clinical and managerial space and play in both settings with your power to hold the tension in integrating good and bad, past and present.

The part in us which colludes with embodying the "deviant" for other treatment modalities, so that they can define their own sense of "normality", is connected with our "idealism". We want to solve all conflicts by dialogue and like to deny the vital function of power and hierarchy in stabilising a Health System or a therapeutic relationship. Individually and collectively, we tend by training to be inhibited about action, which is what power and play have in common. Doing, acting and imposing our will on others is denigrated and only being, supporting and empathising is idealised. This is a split that lends us an inauthentic rather than a real sense of authority in the presence of other power holders. They sense that we split off and project our aggressive parts into them, and as they are less neurotic about inequality and fairness, they feel that they can impose their will on us. As long as we over-identify with being victims, we will be condemned to carry the fear of death and a sense of existential threat on behalf of everyone else. We therefore need to take some power back from the others, the managers and politicians, by consciously refusing to carry their insecurity. We can use our deep knowledge of what is inside and outside, and what happens in the potential space between me and you and us and them more consciously and playfully in meetings as well as in therapy.

Transitions and liminal time

In transitional periods, like the current modernisation drive within our Health Systems, social relationships are not embedded in secure social structures but "suspended" in "liminal time" between an old and a new order. It is a bit like carnival, when social differences between people tend to be forgotten or reversed in a shared feeling of communion; when normal power relations are playfully suspended and the world is turned upside down. Anthropologists identify this as the period when humans try to be in touch with the super-natural, indulge in magical thinking and when "miracles of healing may occur but miracles of disaster also" (Leach, 1986). In concrete terms, this happens in a situation when human groups flee into omnipotence in order to deny their fear of losing a sense of integrity and identity because "the times are changing". This describes the impression I pick up in the Psychotherapy Communities across Europe. The image I hold for what is going on at present in Psychotherapy Departments is that they are involved in power play and that the game is a matter of life and death.

Power play is a technical term used to describe a situation where one ice hockey team is under attack from the opposing side because it has lost a player who has committed a foul and been sent to the sin-bin. Power play means being under siege, threatened with losing the game or a winning position. It is an apt metaphor for what is going on between politicians, health managers and psychotherapists. In the Health Systems I work in as a consultant and supervisor, in the UK, Denmark, Switzerland, Germany, Australia and New Zealand, there is a sense that the modernisation agenda of the neo-liberal state has put our community of practitioners into a power play situation, facing oppositional forces which always seem more likely to walk away as winners. We feel powerless and unable to play, as the opposing team is in our eyes, no longer a playmate but a spoilsport.

Consciously and unconsciously, the Health Systems in Europe are experienced as persecuting and we feel unable to work in a care-free sense with our commitment to dialogue, reason and integration because collectively, we feel trapped in a primitive, split universe which requires us to engage in restoring the capacity to play before we can engage in exchanges with the managers and politicians on a more mature basis. Just as Winnicott (1971) argued that patients with personality disorders need first to learn to play with the analyst before analysis proper can begin, we are faced with the task of recovering our capacity to hold on to the power to play within the Health System. We must therefore separate from the wish for organisational containment and adapt to the liminal and transitional period we are in. We are in organisations that are no longer neurotic and containing but suffer from permanent transition, re-engineering and leadership changes. In other words, we hope in vain for adequate organisational holding structures, and nurturing and re-assuring experiences with managerial "parent figures". We need to risk getting involved in developing an "environmental mother" that can be experienced by us and the managers as a potential space where power and powerlessness can be played with in a benign, rather than malignant way.

We can take it upon ourselves to transform a traumatising context of Health Reform into a potential space for exchange and the re-empowerment of our professional community. We are in the same situation as patients who come to us. We are in a deep enough crisis to finally want to look at what we have got ourselves into. Only we possess the power to look at what we are denying and have colluded with. To paraphrase Winnicott (1965), not the analyst but the patient has the power to know the inside of the Analysand; the power of the analyst lies in limiting the number of interpretations and in creating an environment in which both analyst and Analysand can play. If we substitute patient for bureaucratic tormentor and analyst for psychotherapist, sitting in a meeting with people who have power but are too concrete and boring to play, then we have a picture of facing the choice, at every point in a meeting, to become a victim, a bystander or a perpetrator. All three positions need to be taken up, over and over again. This we can only do, as I suggested, when we give ourselves permission to educate the organisational parents and stop being overly dependent on them in the position of the needy child. The way we tend to see power gets in the way of engaging more consciously in such a power play. If we are to re-cover our own sense of play and power in relation to our own profession and the outside world, we must try and resist thinking so concretely about power. In my view, power is a quality of inter-dependence and in-betweenness and I have written about this with colleagues in a recent book called *Living Leadership—a practical guide for ordinary heroes* (Binney et al., 2005).

What is the implication of seeing power as located in the relationship we have with each other? First, that we accept that history is not just made by great individuals who wrestle the rest of a powerless mass into shape and submit it to their will. Second, that in normal times social change does not follow the logic of historical inevitability. Third, that social, economic and political change, just like in individual therapy and group analysis, rests on the quality of the relationships between the social actors involved. The process of interaction can therefore be used playfully to attain a degree of relative autonomy in relation to the aims and wishes of the power-players and their potential victims. In other words, we co-create the process of exchange which can develop into a master-servant, parent-child, and child-parent or servant-master relationship. Like the Good Soldier Schweijk (Hasek, 1972) or Sanyo Panache in Don Quixote (Cervantes, 2006) we can be in the inferior role whilst taking charge of our superiors, without them losing face. Fourth, that interdependence means that we are neither free nor entirely un-free to influence and shape events and outcomes. This means that no-one is all powerful or all powerless. In other words, this way of conceptualising power brings us nearer to our way of thinking: getting from a dyadic and split universe of goodies and baddies into a world of triangulation, ambivalence and limited self-determination in interdependence with others who have the power to play with us, help us play or become spoilsports. We can only recover our ability to feel more powerful in relation to others and playful about our own self-ideal when we accept that we are both powerful and powerless. Psychotherapists, by training, have learnt to tolerate this state of ambivalence and not knowing. This is the weapon we have; let's use it more knowingly and more "offensively" in the game of surviving repeated Health Reforms.

Playful use of power

If we never own the perpetrator, the power player in us, how are we to cope with the power play in the modernising Health Systems? We become as powerless as we fear and forget that power is relational, not a quality of evil located in isolated individuals as opposed to other social isolates who are their playthings. Playing, for Winnicott (1971), was the ultimate achievement in self-development and in the therapeutic encounter, so why not between managers and therapists in negotiations about jobs, resources and the definition of what is good or bad therapy? Winnicott discovered play in the 1930s when everyone else worshipped power and the survival of the fittest. This pattern of reducing everything to good and evil, power and powerlessness is repeating itself, and we are the ideal sub-group to act as a location point in the social unconscious for "remembering" what life is really about beyond control, fear and blind obedience to power. The paradox is that we need to meet our apparent oppressors with our own capacity for play and counter-power. Playing has a time and a place and in a meeting with managers or governmental agencies, it is that moment when the group gets stuck and the apparent power holder feels lost and paralysed. At such a moment, relationships stop being hierarchical and can be replaced by peer exchanges on a lateral level where we are all human beings, siblings sharing the same sandpit or playing field. It is at such moments that psychotherapists can make a difference and restore the capacity to link power and play in the presence of other role-players in a shared social space.

Johan Huizinga, the Dutch historian, thought that humans are playful beings and that play was in us before culture evolved (Huizinga, 1963). Play is therefore a sacred rather than a profane human activity. Play is located beyond such binary oppositions as rational and irrational, truthful and untruthful, good and evil, functional and dysfunctional. Huizinga's arguments arose out of the work of the great German sociologist Max Weber (Weber, 1906). In his analysis of modernisation processes, he came to the conclusion that all attempts to rationalise, audit and control the world of work are mathematically rooted in "sacred ideas" and have a religious purpose. By "cleaning" up the world, by progressively "disenchanting" parts of everyday life with an extra-ordinary and magical quality, like psychotherapy, through "outcome research" and demands for economic value, the modernisers want to make the seemingly irrational rational and become the embodiment of secular salvation. This attempt to purify and rationalise the world through the expulsion of magic and play, generates, in Weber's view, an inner need for the opposite. He predicted a return of the irrational in everyday life and in politics as a consequence of the attempt to reform the world and define it as inadequate. Psychotherapists know this mechanism as the return of the repressed, which becomes visible in groups and society when someone develops a valence for embodying and personifying that which has socially been made unconscious by the current holders of power, their followers and bystanders. By hanging on to the knowledge that play is sacred, we can as a profession, become the location point in the matrix of a meeting with other professionals and managers for a kind of counter-power, in opposition to the modernisers and their "repressed" wish to be holier than everyone else. If we do not make this choice consciously, someone else will eventually embody these repressed values associated with play and magic unconsciously, in order to make public that even in a secular and modernised society, there are still values and human needs present that are more archetypal than any political and professional fashion. The irrational and religious element in the current wave of reforms is the attempt to find the magic key to making a Health System accountable and psychotherapy a guaranteed success.

Reality will eventually reveal the self-destructive nature of these high-minded ideals and in the meantime, we will have a hard time, feeling helpless whilst attempting to retain our capacity to think and play. Who else but us has the training to tolerate and work with this tension in a mature way? Play deals with the uncontrollable nature of reality by providing a space for tension, uncertainty, risk, gain and loss. As part of the adult world, play emerges at unpredictable times, and I have suggested that we use our capacity to tolerate uncertainty and use transitional spaces in a range of contexts, not just during the sacred therapy hour. To play with Weber's (1906) images, we have the power to let the profane into the sacred therapy space in order to survive by complying with enough of the modernisation demands to not become extinct. We also have it within us to use our knowledge of children's play and the power of unconscious processes in such profane spaces as team meetings.

What does it take to seize moments of everyday life and turn them into "temporary play spaces" to enhance our reputation as serious power brokers in processes designed to work out how best to do things in Health Care Organisation? It is by having the courage to own the child within the professional adult and demonstrate to others that survival does not depend on a withdrawal into the position of the sulking child, but in the ability to use the temporary suspension of normal business in a playful way in order to integrate the loss of past gains, engage with current difficulties and maintain the hope that mastery of an uncertain future is a definite possibility.

Conclusion

Play therapy has become a way for children to work things through. Albert Einstein thought that children learn to think through play and he called serious adult thinking 'Gedankenexperimente'; experiments in the mind by playing through a series of ideas beyond what we already know (Bettelheim, 1987). In other words, the serious intellectual task of working out how the world works depends on the presence of a 'Spielraum', plenty of room for thinking and a space for working things through in a free and associative way, without the interference of authority figures, rigid formulas and procedures. It is clear that the modernisers are intent on controlling the playroom of psychotherapists. Therefore, it is up to us to be selfish enough to use the play spaces that emerge in our work environments to secure our own position and future.

Erik Erikson argued that the adult who is alive to his or her need for continuity and change throughout life, draws on the inner capacity to play at work like a child, knowing that an adult can never be as free in play as his or her younger self (Hoare, 2002). The adult, who in Erikson's view is capable of negotiating the transitions in the life cycle with the help of play at work, is able to integrate the lost past and self-regulate the fear of the future. The professional adult who retains this capacity for play, can explore "new identity elements" and locate them in a changed idea of his or her belonging community. By being open to Einstein's Gedankenexperimente, Erikson thought that such adults begin to see where these newly imagined experiences might lead, and this reduces their levels of paranoid anxiety and helps them regain an inner sense of power and control over their destiny in an unpredictable and unknowable future.

To conclude, Winnicott (1971) located playing between inside and outside; I have located power between the self and the other. I hope that these ideas can help readers to re-connect the inter-dependence of play and power and open a space to find strategies for using play power as a counter to the power play we all experience at present in our respective Health Systems.

CHAPTER EIGHT

Research in psychoanalytic psychotherapy with children— an enterprise in need of power?

Karen Vibeke Mortensen

The suggestion that a whole field of research is suffering from a lack of power may sound quite provocative. Is it justified? Although it may be somewhat pushed to the extremes, I think the facts show it to be true. Knowledge about psychoanalytic psychotherapy with children is lagging behind, not only behind what is known about other forms of psychotherapy, but also behind the corresponding knowledge of psychoanalytic psychotherapy with adults.

As I will explain, there may be a number of different reasons for this. Some of these reasons are of an instrumental character, due to the technical complications connected with research in psychoanalytic psychotherapy and with children, but more irrational, emotional and attitudinal factors may also play a part, factors that are characteristic of the whole field of clinical child psychology and not confined only to psychotherapy research.

The present state of research in child psychotherapy

Research in psychotherapy is traditionally divided into case studies and large-scale quantitative studies, this holding true for research in

145

psychoanalytic psychotherapy with children as well. My concentration on systematic, large-scale, quantitative studies in this chapter is not due to a disregard for case studies or to an understanding of them as irrelevant, less necessary, or less empirically based than the large-scale studies. They are, however, not accepted as the kind of evidence-based research that society wants. Society asks us, justly, if it gets value for money when it pays for psychotherapy, and we cannot escape this demand for quantitative and large-scale research. Public health authorities use such studies as evidence for or against the approval of psychotherapeutic treatment.

It is a fact that much more research has been carried out on psychoanalytic psychotherapy with adults than with children and adolescents. In their book on research in child and adolescent psychotherapy, Boëtius and Berggren (2000) make it clear that there is a substantial lack of studies in psychodynamic and psychoanalytic psychotherapy as carried out in clinical practice. They estimated that research in psychotherapy with children and adolescents lagged more than 10 years behind the corresponding research with adults. This viewpoint was supported by Windaus in Berlin (2006) in his presentation of a summary on the position and outcome of psychotherapy research in Europe in the child and adolescent field. He concluded that compared to research in adult psychotherapy, analytic therapy research for children and adolescents was still in its early stages, and ended by quoting Kronmüller & Hartmann (1997) saying that, "There is a huge lack of empirical research, that evidence for the efficacy for psychoanalytical children and adolescents therapy is missing, that empirically oriented psychoanalytical process research for children and adolescents exists only to a limited extent and that the construction of analytically oriented instruments still is in a developmental stage" (Windaus, 2006).

The British reports by Kennedy (2004) and Kennedy & Midgley (2007), which are based on very thorough database analysis, conclude that although there are quite a number of studies of the effects of psychotherapy with children and adolescents, the vast literature becomes a "minute literature" if only the studies that examine therapy with clinical samples and in clinical settings are counted. The authors also conclude that perhaps the greatest limitation of contemporary therapy research is the paucity of studies that attempt to explain why and how treatment works. Unless an understanding of the psychotherapy process can be incorporated into investigations of treatment outcome, progress will be limited. Although the study of the process of psychotherapy with adults has developed rapidly during the last twenty years, progress in the empirical study of work with children has lagged behind. They distinguish between:

1. Exploratory studies,
2. Hypotheses testing studies, and
3. Theory development, i.e., studies which examine the links between specific psychotherapy processes and theories of change.

Most of the existing studies fall within the first category, which, as they say, is to be expected in a fairly undeveloped area of research.

Why is this so? There seem to be a number of reasons. As mentioned, some are quite rational and have to do with the complexities of clinical work with children, including psychotherapy research. Other reasons may be less rational and are not confined to research in psychotherapy, but influence the whole field of clinical child psychology.

Scientist, practitioner or both?

The ideal of the scientist-practitioner was introduced by the American Psychological Association as early as 1947 (Shakow et al., 1947), and quickly attained international recognition. However, practice has shown that it has, to a greater degree, remained an ideal which has been difficult to realize. Clinical practitioners are often criticized for being uninterested in and uninformed of what research has to offer, and for letting their work be led more by intuition and earlier practice than by hard facts. Many practicing psychotherapists will more or less guiltily acknowledge that there may be some truth in this. There may be several, more or less acceptable, reasons for it, however many practitioners feel that the information offered by research is tedious and dull and offers little new knowledge that is relevant for practice.

This criticism from researchers to practitioners is well-known; criticism in the other direction is perhaps not so common. Nevertheless, it is just as important that researchers are trained in psychotherapy as that practitioners are well-informed of research. If this is not the case, there is a very real risk that their research may actually be irrelevant. Researchers who work in "pure" research environments run the risk of choosing subjects for their research which are easy to handle and understand but which, because of their limited complexity, are not very relevant to practice. It is generally accepted that studies carried out under experimental laboratory conditions are artefacts, since factors such as randomisation, allocation to control groups, and manualisation of the therapy, distort the assessment of efficacy under field conditions. Participants are often selected according to disorder, with no comorbidity, and with subjects recruited by, for instance, advertisement in places that are not actual treatment settings. They suffer usually from less complex problems and have a better family background than most clinical patients. The kind and length of treatment offered often differs from general practice, and the psychotherapists are not always sufficiently trained. There seems to be agreement that it is necessary to implement controlled efficacy studies in real care settings in order to obtain results that are comparable to treatment as carried out in practice. There is, therefore, good reason to ask for research done by researchers who are well-trained clinicians and who work in real clinical settings.

One argument against research in clinical settings concerns the difficulty of obtaining control groups as for ethical reasons you cannot very well leave some children untreated. This problem can be overcome, however, through the establishment of parallel treatment groups with variations in treatment parameters instead of an untreated group as control.

One of the difficulties of this requirement of double competence is the fact that it makes enormous demands on the scientist-practitioner. You have to be a specialist in your clinical field and to have had a good deal of practice to have enough understanding to do meaningful research; on top of that, you have to be trained in research. The training of child psychotherapists has often taken place in private institutions or organizations without a basis in research, and unlike university teachers, the teachers of child psychotherapy are not qualified as researchers. So role models for the scientist-practitioner-model may be lacking. Specialization in psychoanalytic child psychotherapy requires long and costly training which, in some countries at least, is paid for by the candidates themselves. What is needed are positions that offer training in psychotherapy and in research at the same time, without extra costs for the student. Society will get value for money by offering such possibilities, as some countries already do.

Organizational complications

It is ideal, therefore, if research can be done in institutions and organizations which actually have clinical work as their main occupation. Such institutions, however, are usually under pressure for high productivity. The work load is maximal and the administration rarely values research, which is seen rather as something that steals time and resources from practical work, as opposed to being an advantage. There may well be the demand for research, but it has to be done somewhere else.

It is true that research takes a lot of time and resources. Good research, however, presupposes the existence of a research-culture and an environment where research is welcomed, seen as necessary and important. Good research is a creative enterprise and requires space; space for imagination and play with ideas and thoughts. It is very difficult to do research if you work in a place where there is little knowledge of the necessary conditions for research and where few people have an understanding of it, not least the professional qualifications to do it. An isolated researcher in an institution without a tradition for research runs the risk of developing serious identity problems, of feeling unwanted and unimportant, and perhaps even of being more or less excluded from the community. Although an institution that is inexperienced in research may herald the introduction of a project as exciting and prestigious, it may quickly tire of the daily demands and feel frustrated by the long time that may elapse before any results can be seen. The introduction of a research project into a treatment institution with no prior experience of research is no small enterprise; it has far-reaching consequences for all aspects of the institution and requires changes in attitude and practice to a much greater degree than may have been anticipated. It is not easy to find a proper balance between clinical practice and research.

A factor which further complicates research at this point in time are the many changes to formal organizational structure that take place, not least in the social field. Research requires at least that the institution or the environment where the research takes place, exists during the time when the research is going on. A further helpful factor is that it does not change radically during the process. Today however, many institutions are not established as permanent units, but are based on time-limited grants and funds. They often direct their efforts towards special groups of children or adolescents who have caught public awareness, such as adolescents with eating disturbances or cutting behaviour, but when the grants stop and the community should take over, they are often closed down again. Such a scenario is not facilitative of research. In such a context, only small projects with limited information are possible, but that is not what is needed. What is needed, are projects that continue over time and give long-term information. The scarcity of stable institutions makes this difficult.

Psychiatric institutions usually have a tradition for research, which is seen as a natural part of the training of doctors. The social welfare sector has a very different history and different traditions. It has a history of taking care of people who are poor and have all kinds of social problems and, originally, concentrated its efforts mainly on various forms of social support or control. Only later were psychological interventions, such as psychotherapy, added to the repertoire. Before this, the social sector had no tradition for academically trained people, except amongst administrative staff. Nonetheless, many of the existing treatment institutions for children are now placed in the social system. Psychotherapists and other staff groups who are trained in the treatment of children have been introduced, but they are rarely placed in positions where they have sufficient power to decide when or how research should be undertaken, if at all. It has been customary to search for sociological and statistical data in social research, but there is little tradition in the use of psychological data. Outcome of treatment and other interventions is often measured in concrete results such as numbers of criminal acts and similar obvious forms of behaviour, rather than in psychological changes. The social system has a substantial need for augmentation and sophistication of its understanding of the psychological processes behind the development of psychic and social problems and the interventions applied. It needs, for example, to see that it is possible to grasp and understand some of the underlying psychological factors behind the so-called "negative social inheritance", a popular concept in the debate on children's problems. This is a very large and rich, undeveloped area of research, which needs cultivation and some initiative on our part.

Complications inherent in the work with children

So far, the complications of research in psychoanalytic child psychotherapy have had to do with training of researchers, organizational circumstances, and the function of the social system; but other complications follow more directly from the use of children as subjects of research. It has been mentioned that research in psychotherapy with adults has progressed more than the analogous research with children. So why are the results from the adult field not just extrapolated to children? This is not possible because, as stated by Kennedy & Midgley (2007), the process of child psychotherapy is quite distinct from work with adults.

A very important difference consists of children's dependence on their parents, legally, physically and psychologically. This factor has consequences for many aspects of both treatment and research, for establishment of contract, assessment, treatment alliance and form of treatment. Parents enter into the process from the very start. It is necessary to obtain their permission to get access to the children you want to study; it is not possible to establish contracts with the children themselves.

Children are, to only a limited degree, able to describe their problems directly in language. They have to be well into adolescence before they can adequately describe feelings and thoughts about their situation in words. This means that easy research instruments such as questionnaires or interviews are not suitable. Instead, indirect methods such as psychological tests or information from others such as family and teachers are necessary. In tests or play-observation, the information is given in symbolic form. Such information is often of a character which necessitates interpretation and therefore clinical experience to be adequately understood. This is one of the factors that make thorough clinical training so important.

Information from relatives or teachers has often been shown to deviate from information from children or adolescents themselves (Fonagy & Target, 1996; Cantwell & Rutter, 1994; Achenbach & Rescorla, 2007). Both factors add greatly to the complexity of reliability and validity.

In addition, the parents are not involved only at the start of the research. Much research has shown the importance of the parents' participation in their children's treatment (Kennedy & Midgley, 2007). There is even evidence that children's families can show increased disturbance if their children are treated without the family being involved (Szapocznik et al., 1989; Trowell et al., 2007).

Process research in the field of adult psychotherapy has increasingly come to emphasize the quality of the patient-therapist relationship itself as a fundamental factor in therapeutic change. However, in child psychotherapy, not only is the alliance with the child important, the alliance with the parents can be the crucial factor both in the establishment and the maintenance of child psychotherapy.

The inclusion of parents at all stages of the treatment process, from the start of contact to the end, is a costly, time-consuming and complicating factor, adding greatly to the complexity of the whole design, the number of variables and the understanding of the results. Not least, process research is much more complex than if only a single patient-therapist relation is involved.

Problems of diagnostics

The slower development of knowledge about children as opposed to adults is, however, not confined just to the domain of research, but also characterizes other areas of work. It is true, for instance, in the diagnostic field, diagnoses for children were introduced later than diagnoses for adults; there are fewer of them and they are based on less research than are those for adults. Neither reliability nor validity is sufficient (Cantwell & Rutter, 1994). The present diagnostic systems, ICD-10 and DSM-IV, contribute much to the difficulties in doing meaningful research. Our instruments govern our thinking and conceptualization to a much greater degree than is often realized. Those of us who have worked with children and adolescents over many years, will have had the experience of working with several successive diagnostic systems. It is really interesting to see how one way of categorization which has been in use for years is discarded, literally from one day to the next, and replaced by a different system, which is then, with great enthusiasm, heralded as the "correct" system, supplying us with reliable and valid truth. Diagnoses that have been used for years are suddenly old-fashioned, and it does not take long before they are forgotten. An example of this could be the concept of borderline states in children, which is now mainly replaced by the diagnoses of Aspergers syndrome and autistic spectrum disorders. Earlier, there was much interest in, and qualified therapeutic work carried out with children with borderline disturbances. There was interest in exploration of their family situation and attempts at understanding the psychodynamics of these children and their families. But since the change of diagnosis to Aspergers syndrome and autistic spectrum disorders, these children are regarded by most people as basically brain-damaged or born with certain deficits which are often not regarded as accessible for psychotherapy. As demonstrated in this book, psychotherapeutic work with them and their families exists, but it has become scarce.

Diagnostic concepts are not just names; they represent whole universes of thinking about how to understand and treat mental problems. With the introduction of ICD-10, there was even a change from a partly humanistic to a purely natural scientific understanding, which is a very radical shift. Often, the full consequences of changes that on the surface look small, such as a change of name, are only slowly understood to their full extent.

It is paradoxical that at a time when we know more than ever about early disorders of relationships and their significance for psychopathology, a diagnostic system is used which is based solely on symptomatology. Not only that, the system is quite consistently focused on genetic, biochemical and neurophysiologic explanations and discards even well established empirical knowledge of, for example, the connections between family factors and children's behavioural problems. In 1997, the Danish doctor Aksel Bertelsen wrote that the introduction of ICD-10 should not lead to a fear of a mechanistic impoverishment of psychiatry (Bertelsen, 1997). He must have felt a need to calm himself, I suppose, but I am sorry to say that what he said is a very precise description of what has actually happened. Danish child psychiatry has changed very much since the introduction of ICD-10. The assessment of families and work with them has been much reduced, as has treatment of the children. Child psychiatry work is under great pressure, partly due to a lack of psychological treatment facilities for children. Information which goes beyond what is necessary to make a diagnosis will easily be felt as superfluous, particularly when time and resources only offer very limited possibilities for treatment anyway. It is striking how very fast these changes happen and how difficult it is, not to say impossible, to keep valuable aspects of earlier ways of thinking alive. In addition, many professionals show a surprisingly great respect, almost reverence, for natural science as if that by itself ensures good quality.

The diagnoses of the present systems are easy to count, quantify and treat statistically. But the fact that children are under continuous development makes the use of symptom-based diagnoses as criteria unsatisfactory. In children, symptoms can change with age and development but still be expressions of the same underlying problem. The reverse can also be true in that seemingly similar symptoms can cover quite different problems. Because children are under continuous development, it is necessary to be able to distinguish between ordinary age development and specific treatment related changes. That also makes quantitative measures that stand alone unsatisfactory; they have to be supplemented with descriptions of qualitative changes that can be related directly to the treatment processes.

Good research with children, therefore, has to go under the surface of symptomatology to pick up on the important variables. Already in 1994, Cantwell & Rutter warned against the use of diagnoses alone as a sufficient basis for intervention. "A diagnostic term or even a multiaxial set of codings cannot provide a sufficient summary of all that is clinically important. Classificatory terms provide a handy summary for communication but, in clinical practice, they need to be supplemented by diagnostic formulations that bring out what is individual and special in the problems presented by the particular patient ... . They provide a useful general guide but not all children with a particular diagnosis require the same treatment or the same service. It is necessary that services should be tailored to individual needs rather than provided on the basis of diagnostic pigeon-holing" (Cantwell & Rutter, 1994, p. 17). Personality factors and psychological variables need to be operationalized if they are to be useful, but there is not yet consensus about how best to describe children's psychological difficulties.

Psychoanalysis has not cared much about classification. In 1966, Anna Freud made her diagnostic profile for children, but since then, little interest has been given to this field, despite her warnings that it was necessary. We could, of course, say that as psychoanalysts we do not care about official diagnostics, that we establish our own understanding of the problems based on our own frame of reference. But in saying this we would be neglecting the fact that the need for classification is a legal one, and when we abandon the field, we leave it open to others with other world views. We have let others take over and we are now confronted with a system which has all the power of being the official one. While professionals may know about the weaknesses of the diagnostic system, which surprisingly many of them actually don't, lay persons such as administrators or politicians can do nothing but trust the official system, and it is difficult to be heard if you try to introduce another understanding which is both more complicated and which does not have the weight of an official stamp.

Why are child workers so powerless?

But why is it so much more attractive to think in terms of symptoms and in genetic and biochemical causes, rather than in relational terms? Bowlby (1973) drew attention to an important reason when he talked about the powerful, but unacknowledged tendency for collusion between professionals and parents about not blaming the parents. Professionals who insist on the necessity of an assessment of family functioning and on the possibility of offering psychotherapy both to children and to their families, are quite often met with the question whether they really want to blame the parents? It is as if blame and responsibility are muddled up. It is acceptable to talk about the possibly good influences parents can have on their children but not to include the other side of the coin, the possibly not-so-good influences they/we may have.

Another difficulty is I think, connected with the low prestige of work with children. When talking about psychiatry in general, we mean adult psychiatry, and when talking about psychoanalysis, without further specification, adult analysis is meant. Children have a minority status, almost in the same way that women used to have, when speaking about people in general and afterwards, mentioning some special traits that characterized women. We talk of subspecialties when we talk of child analysis, child psychology or child psychiatry.

Already in 1970, Anna Freud wondered why psychoanalysts showed so little interest in the opportunity, through child analysis, to confirm or disconfirm their hypotheses and on the whole, at their distance from child analysis "almost as if it is an inferior type of work" (p. 211). Her statement seems to have been supported by the development of clinical psychology which, in many countries, has left children with far too few treatment possibilities. There is, of course, a connection between the number of treatment facilities for children and the amount of research taking place.

From the beginning, part of the reason for the low status of child psychotherapy might have had to do with the fact that neither Anna Freud nor Melanie Klein had academic training and so lacked the associated prestige. Their lack of academic training was probably again related to their sex. Melanie Klein originally wanted to become a doctor but gave up her plans and married early. Anna Freud's conflicts between her role as a woman, a scientist and a psychotherapist are well-known (Young-Bruehl, 1989).

It is also a fact that work with children in society at large, does not have the same power and prestige that society grants work with adults. This is obvious from the way teachers and pedagogues are valued and paid. There still seems to be some support for the attitude that caretaking of children is something that does not require much training; after all, women have done so for centuries without having to go to school to learn it. The fact that child analysis and child psychology and psychiatry are predominantly female occupations, unfortunately, does not add to their prestige.

In addition, over the years, psychoanalysis has often been under attack as being old-fashioned and antiquated and not able to compete with shorter, more effective and evidence-based treatments. As a psychoanalyst or child analyst, it is not rare to be met with surprise and scepticism at your choice of work.

It is my impression that as psychoanalytic child psychotherapists, we often feel great humility towards our work. We know how complicated and difficult it can be to help children overcome their problems and we realize that there are still very many things we do not know or understand. Furthermore, we probably all recognize the moments of despair and hopelessness that almost always seem to occur in psychotherapies with difficult children or, of long duration.

When these feelings combine with the above-mentioned feelings of inferiority connected to work with children in general, it is perhaps no wonder that we tend to keep a low profile.

What can be done?

But perhaps our modesty is disproportionate. Much research in other kinds of psychotherapy suffers from similar shortcomings to the research in psychoanalytic psychotherapy; many studies of cognitive behaviour therapy are done with artificial groups of non-clinic patients with no co-morbidity, a lack of control groups, or insufficiently defined outcome parameters. Neither are long-term effects sufficiently demonstrated (Vandborg, 2007). If our modesty is so all encompassing that it hinders relevant information from being brought forward, it is more harmful than commendable. In addition to our therapeutic skill, we have considerable knowledge about children which is important to pass on. We should not forget that through our work as psychotherapists, we have singularly good opportunities to see and understand some of the circumstances and factors in families, in the living conditions of children, and in society at large, that are of importance for the development of good psychic health as well as of psychopathology.

Parents and official authorities need to be informed that children who have problems need help in order that this help can be given, but also that it takes time and knowledge to provide it. We should not withhold our knowledge that children are not helped by being diagnosed by symptom-based diagnoses, but that much more knowledge is needed about their total functioning and the conditions under which they live, if adequate help is going to be offered to them.

Although the official diagnostic systems are still dominant, other diagnostic instruments have been developed which rely on a much more differentiated and deeper understanding of what is needed to make a satisfactory diagnosis, and which may help prepare the way for more useful and relevant forms of classification. The Diagnostic Classification: 0–3 (DC: 0–3) (Zero-to-Three, 1994) was published back in 1994 and in 2006 the Psychodynamic Diagnostic Manual (PDM Task Force, 2006) was edited. In the DC: 0–3, many aspects of the small child's functioning are considered crucial for a diagnosis, and the relationships between the child and his caregivers are also classified. In the PDM, one part of the manual is for adults, another for children and adolescents and a third for infants. In the section for children and adolescents, the assessment starts with a description of a number of the child's mental functions and personality tendencies, such as processing capacities, engagement in relationships, emotional patterns and behaviour tendencies. Both systems underline the necessity of assessing patterns and relations and not just symptoms.

Many tools of observation aim at the assessment of global patterns and qualities of interaction. Relationships cannot be assessed through observation of specific acts, because the quality of the acting is of such vital importance that it determines the meaning of it. The specific details often derive their meaning from the background of the total pattern and this sets grave limits on the use of quantitative scorings in favour of more qualitative ones. The use of such instruments often requires both general clinical experience and specific training in the use of the instrument. This may be costly and time-consuming. Operationalized, however, these factors offer a good basis for the description of structural changes and thus for psychotherapy research. Although, as mentioned before, there is not yet a consensus about the best possible operationalization of the relevant personality variables to be used in research, quite a few instruments have been developed which can be used and which are both reliable and valid. A number of these are described by Kennedy & Midgley (2007).

We should not be reluctant to share our knowledge that the close relations in the life of a child are of vital importance for his ability to thrive, and that treatment is insufficient when directed only towards the removal of symptoms, in that parents and other key-persons have to be involved.

In many countries, there is very little public knowledge about the existence of psychoanalytic child psychotherapy and about what it can do. Although it is true that there is still not enough research, it has been demonstrated and empirically shown that psychoanalytic treatment can help; it can even help children with severe and early personality problems which are not easily helped by other methods. We need not be afraid also of stressing the need for long-term treatment; ambulatory treatment, even of long duration, is very cheap, compared to other forms of intervention. A very simple calculation shows that you can get almost two years of twice-weekly ambulatory psychotherapy and corresponding work with the parents for the same price as one month's hospitalization in a psychiatric child department.

We have an immense task of information dissemination in front of us, towards the general public and towards the specific systems of society that take care of children and their families. Perhaps the most important step forward would be to secure the establishment of treatment units for children and adolescents in the psychology departments of universities. This would provide opportunities for experimentation with, and development of, various models of treatment and for long-term research of good quality. This would secure opportunities for the training of psychotherapists/researchers to a high standard.

Children do not have the power to speak for themselves, at least not in a direct language that is understood by everyone. Those of us who work with children must try to lend them our voices.

REFERENCES

Achenbach, T.M. & Rescorla, L.A. (2007). *Multicultural Understanding of Child and Adolescence Psychopathology.* New York: Guilford Press.

Akhtar, S. (1999). *Inner Torment: Living between Conflict and Fragmentation.* Jason Aronson Inc.

Auster, P. (1982). *The Invention of Solitude.* New York: Penguin Books.

Balint, M. (1951). On Love and Hate. In: Evans, W.N. *Primary Love and Psychoanalytic Technique.* (1965). London: Tavistock Publications.

Balint, M. (1968). *The Basic Fault. Therapeutic Aspects of Regression.* London - New York: Tavistock Publications, 1979.

Barnett, B. (2006). Foreword. In: M. Lanyado & A. Horne, *A Question of Technique – Independent approaches with children and adolescents* (pp. xi–xv). Hove, UK: Routledge, 2006.

Bateson, G. (1979). *Mind and Nature; a Necessary Unity.* London: Wildwood House.

Bell, D. (2001). Projective identification. In: C. Bronstein (Ed.), *Kleinian Theory: A Contemporary Perspective* (pp. 125–147). London: Whurr Publishers.

Berman, E. (2004). *Impossible Training—The Relational View of Psychoanalytic Education.* Hillsdale NJ, London: The Analytic Press.

161

Bertelsen, A. (1997). ICD-10, en ny psykiatri. *Månedsskrift for praktisk lægegerning, 75*: 91–97.

Bettelheim, B. (1987). *A Good Enough Parent*. London: Thames and Hudson.

Binney, G., Wilke, G. & Williams, C. (2005). *Living Leadership, a Practical Guide for Ordinary Heroes*. Harlow: Financial Times and Prentice Hall.

Bion, W.R. (1959). Attacks on Linking. In: E.B. Spillius (Ed.), *Melanie Klein Today: Developments in Theory and Practice. Volume 1: Mainly Theory* (pp. 87–101). London: Routledge 1988.

Bion, W.R. (1962a). A Theory of Thinking. In: E.B. Spillius, (Ed.), *Melanie Klein Today: Developments in theory and practice. Vol. 1: Mainly Theory* (pp. 178–186). London: Routledge, 1988.

Bion, W.R. (1962b). *Learning from Experience*. London: Karnac Books, 1991.

Bion, W.R. (1967a). Notes on Memory and Desire. In: E.B. Spillius (Ed.), *Melanie Klein Today: Developments in Theory and Practice. Volume 2: Mainly Practice* (pp. 17–21). London: Routledge, 1988.

Bion, W.R. (1967b). *Second Thoughts: Selected Papers on Psycho-Analysis*. London: Heinemann Medical; Maresfield Library (1984).

Bion, W.R. (1970). *Attention and Interpretation*. London: Tavistock.

Black, D.M. (Ed.) (2006). *Psychoanalysis and Religion in the 21st Century. Competitors or Collaborators*. London and New York: Routledge.

Boëtius, S.B. & Berggren, G. (2000). *Forskning om barn- och ungdomspsykoterapi. En kundskabsöversikt*. Stockholm: Ericastiftelsen.

Bollas, C. (1985). Loving Hate. *Annual of Psychoanalysis, 12/13*: 221–373.

Bollas, C. (1987). *The Shadow of the Object: Psychoanalysis of the Unknown Known*. London: Karnac Books.

Bollas, C. (1991). *Forces of Destiny, Psychoanalysis and Human Idiom*. London: Free Association Books.

Bowlby, J. (1973). *Attachment and Loss: Volume 2. Separation, Anxiety and Anger*. New York: Basic Books.

Britton, R.S. (1989). The Missing Link: Parental Sexuality in the Oedipus Situation. In: R. Britton, M. Feldman & E. O'Shaughnessy (Eds.), *The Oedipus Complex Today*. London: Karnac Books.

Britton, R.S. (1992). The Oedipus Situation and the Depressive Position. In: Anderson, R., *Clinical lectures on Klein and Bion*. London and New York: Routledge.

Burgner, M. (1986). The Oedipal Experience: Effects on Development of an Absent Father. *International Journal of Psychoanalysis, 66*: 311–320.

Burman, E. (2005). Contemporary Feminist Contributions to Debates around Gender and Sexuality: From Identity to Performance. *Group Analysis, 38 (1)*: 17–30.

Cantwell, D.P. & Rutter, M. (1994). Classification: Conceptual Issues and Substantive Findings. In: M. Rutter, E. Taylor & L. Hersov, (Eds.), *Child and Adolescent Psychiatry.* Oxford: Blackwell Scientific Publications.

Caper, R. (1996). Play, Experimentation and Creativity. *International Journal Psycho-Analysis, 77*: 859–869.

Caper, R. (1999). *A Mind of One's Own.* London and New York: Routledge.

Casement, P. (1985). *On Learning from the Patient.* London and New York: Tavistock Publications.

Cervantes, M. (2006). *Don Quixote.* Redhill: Naxos AudioBooks.

Clarkin, J.F., Yeomans, F.E. & Kernberg, O.F. (1999). *Psychotherapy for Borderline Personality.* New York: John Wiley & Sons Inc.

Cleve, E. (2004). *From Chaos to Coherence. Psychotherapy with a Little boy with ADHD.* London: Karnac Books.

Coltart, N. (1992). *Slouching Towards Bethlehem.* New York and London: Guilford Press.

Coltart, N. (1993). *How to Survive as a Psychotherapist.* London: Sheldon Press.

Cox, M. & Theilgaard, A. (1987). *Mutative Metaphors in Psychotherapy. The Aeolian Mode.* London: Tavistock.

Davis, M. & Wallbridge, D. (1983). *Boundary and Space: an Introduction to the Work of D.W. Winnicott.* Harmondsworth: Penguin Books.

Edwards, J. (2000). On Being Dropped and Picked up: Adopted Children and their Internal Objects. *Journal of Child Psychotherapy, 26 (3)*: 349–67.

Elias, N. (1991). *Die Gesellschaft der Individuen.* Frankfurt am Main: Suhrkamp Taschenbuch Wissenschaft 974.

Elias, N. & Scotson, J.L. (1993). *Etablierte und Außenseiter.* Frankfurt am Main: Suhrkamp.

Etchegoyen, A. (2002). Psychoanalytic Ideas about Fatherhood. In: Trowell, J. & Etchegoyen, A. *The Importance of Fathers—A Psychoanalytic Re-evaluation.* Hove: Brunner-Routledge.

Fonagy, P., Gergely, G., Jurist, E.L. & Target, M. (2002). *Affect Regulation, Mentalization, and the Development of the Self.* New York: Other Press.

Fonagy, P. & Target, M. (1996). Predictors of Outcome in Child Psychoanalysis: A Retrospective Study of 763 Cases at the Anna Freud Centre. *Journal of the American Psychoanalytic Association, 44 (1)*: 27–77.

Fonagy, P. & Target, M. (2000). Playing with Reality: III. The Persistence of Dual Psychic Reality in Borderline Patients. *International Journal of Psychoanalysis, 81:* 853–873.

Foulkes, S.H. (1990). *Selected papers.* London: Karnac Books.

Fransman, T. (2006). *What is different about listening in psychoanalysis?* Paper given at Scottish Institute of Human Relations and British Institute of Psychoanalysis Conference, Edinburgh October 28th 2006.

Freud, A. (1964) [1967]. Comments on Psychic Trauma. In: *The Writings of Anna Freud, Vol. V: Research at the Hampstead Clinic and Other Papers 1956–1965* (pp. 221–241). New York: International Universities Press, 1969.

Freud, A. (1966). *Normality and Pathology in Childhood.* London: The Hogarth Press.

Freud, A. (1970). Child Analysis as a Subspecialty of Psychoanalysis. In: *The Writings of Anna Freud,* VII: 204–219. New York: International Universities Press.

Freud, S. (1908). *Preface to the Second Edition of The Interpretation of Dreams.* S.E. 4, London: The Hogarth Press.

Freud, S. (1918). *The Case of the Wolf Man. From the History of an Infantile Neurosis.,* S.E. 17, 3. London: The Hogarth Press.

Freud, S. (1921). *Massenpsychologie und Ich-Analyse* (2000) in: Freud, S. Studienausgabe, Fragen der Gesellschaft und Ursprünge der Religion, Frankfurt am Main: Fischer Taschenbuch Verlag, pp. 61–134.

Freud , S. (1923). *The Ego and the Id.* S.E. 19, London: The Hogarth Press.

Freud, S. (1930). *Civilisation and its Discontents.* S.E. 21. London: The Hogarth Press.

Freud , S. (1937). *Constructions in Analysis.* S.E. 23. London: The Hogarth Press.

Freud, S. (1940) [1938]. Splitting of the Ego in the Process of Defence. *Standard Edition, Vol. XXIII,* (pp. 271–278). The Hogarth Press Vintage, 2001.

Friedman, R. (2002). Dream-telling as a Request for Containment in Group Therapy. In: C. Neri, M. Pines & R. Friedman (Eds.), *Dreams in Group Psychotherapy.* International Library of Group Analysis, *18:* 46–66, Jessica Kingsley Publisher.

Friedman, R. (2007). Personal communication.

Gabbard, G.O. (1996). *Love and Hate in the Analytic Setting.* London: Jason Aronson Inc.

Gabbard, G.O. & Wilkinson, S.M. (1994). *Management of Countertransference with Borderline Patients*. Washington, D.C.: American Psychiatric Press.

Gaensburger, T.J. (1995). Trauma in the Preverbal Period. Symptoms, Memories and Developmental Impact. *Psychoanalytic Study of the Child, 50*: 123–149.

Garland, C. (1998). Thinking about Trauma. In: C. Garland (Ed.), *Understanding Trauma: A Psychoanalytic Approach*. London: Tavistock.

Gerhardt, S. (2004). *Why Love Matters. How Affection Shapes a Baby's Brain*. Hove, East Sussex: Routledge.

Gill, H.S. (1991). Internalization of the Absent Father. *International Journal of Psychoanalysis, 72*: 243–252.

Green, A. (1977). The Borderline Concept. In: *On Private Madness* (pp. 60–83). London: The Hogarth Press and The Institute of Psycho-Analysis, 1986.

Green, A. (2000). *Andre Green at the Squiggle Foundation*. London: Karnac Books.

Green, A. (2005). *Play and reflection in Donald Winnicott's writing*. London: Karnac Books.

Green, A. (2009). The construction of the lost father. In: Kalinich, L.J. & Taylor, S.W. (ed.), *The Dead Father—a Psychoanalytic Inquiry*. London and New York: Routledge.

Grünbaum, L. (1997). Psychotherapy with Children in Refugee Families who have Survived Torture: Containment and Understanding of Repetitive Behaviour and Play. *Journal of Child Psychotherapy, 23 (3)*: 437–452.

Grünbaum, L. (2001). Det posttraumatiske mareridt: En vej til integration? *Matrix, 18 (1–2)*: 29–56.

Grünbaum, L. (2006). Gennem stilhed i det tomme rum—børneterapi, tab og traume. In: C.H. Jacobsen, L. Thorgaard & L.L. Petersen (Eds.), *Tilknytning, Tab og Tilblivelse i Psykodynamisk Belysning*. Aalborg Universitetsforlag.

Grünbaum, L. (2007). Supervision af Behandling med Tværkulturelle Problemstillinger. In: C.H. Jacobsen & K.V. Mortensen (Eds.), *Psykodynamisk Supervision*. København: Akademisk forlag.

Grünbaum, L. (2010). The Post-traumatic Nightmare: The via Regia to Unconscious Integration? In: A. Gautier & A. Sabatini (Eds.), *Bearing Witness: Psychoanalytic Work with People Traumatised by Torture and State Violence*. The EFPP Book Series. London: Karnac.

Haag, G. (1985). La Mère et le Bébé dans les Deux Moitiés du Corps. *Neuropsychiatrie de l'Enfance, 33*: 107–114.

Hasek, J. (1972). *Die Abenteuer des Braven Soldaten Schwejk I a. II.* Hamburg: Rororo.

Henry, O. (1904). A Strange Story. In: *The Complete Works of O. Henry.* Authentic ed. Books. Garden City. New York: Garden City, (1937).

Herzog, J.M. (2001). *Father Hunger: Explorations with Adults and Children.* Hillsdale, NJ: Analytic Press.

Hindle, D. (2000). The Merman: Recovering from Early Abuse and Loss. *Journal of Child Psychotherapy, 26 (3)*: 369–91

Hoare, C.H. (2002). *Erikson on Development in Adulthood, New Insights from the Unpublished Papers.* Oxford: Oxford University Press.

Hook, B. (1999). When is a Group not a Circle? *Group Analysis, 32 (3)*: 443–458.

Houde, O. (1997). Rationality in Reasoning: the Problem of Deductive Competence and the Inhibitory Control of Cognition. *Current Psychology of Cognition, 16*: 108–119.

Huizinga, J. (1963). *Homo Ludens: A Study of the Play-Element in Culture.* Florence, KY: Routledge. (reprinted 2000, quotations are according to this edition)

Johnson, J.G., Cohen, P., Brown, J., Smailes, E.M. & Bernstein, D.P. (1999). Childhood Maltreatment Increases Risk for Personality Disorders during Early Adulthood. *Archives General Psychiatry, 56*: 600–607.

Joseph, B. (1985). Transference: the Total Situation. In: E.B. Spillius (Ed.), *Melanie Klein Today. Developments in Theory and Practice. Volume 2: Mainly Practice* (pp. 61–72). London: Routledge, 1988.

Kaplan, S. (2006). Children in Genocide – Extreme Traumatization and the "Affect Propeller". *International Journal of Psychoanalysis, 87*: 725–746.

Kennedy, E. (2004). *Child and Adolescent Psychotherapy: A Systematic Review of Psychoanalytic Approaches.* London: North Central London Strategic Health Authority.

Kennedy, E. & Midgley, N. (2007). *Process and Outcome Research in Child, Adolescent and Parent-Infant Psychotherapy: A Thematic Review.* London: North Central London Strategic Health Authority.

Kernberg, O.F. (1992). *Aggression in Personality Disorder and Perversions.* New York: Jason Aronson Inc.

Kernberg, O.F. (2004). *Aggressivity, Narcissism, and Self-destructiveness in the Psychotherapeutic Relationship.* New Haven and London: Yale University Press.

Kirshner, L.A. (1992). The Absence of the Father. *Journal of American Psychoanalytic Association, 40*: 1117–1121.

Klein, M. (1929). Personification in the Play of Children. *International Journal of Psychoanalysis, 10*: 193–204. In: *The Writings of Melanie Klein* Vol. 1 Love Guilt and Reparation. London: Hogarth, 1975.

Klein, M. (1930). The Importance of Symbol-Formation in the Development of the Ego. In: *Love, Guilt and Reparation and Other Works 1921–1945* (pp. 219–232). London: The Hogarth Press and the Institute of Psycho-Analysis, 1975.

Klein, M. (1957). Envy and gratitude. In: *Envy and Gratitude and Other Works 1946–1963* (pp. 176–235). London: The Hogarth Press and the Institute of Psycho-Analysis, 1975.

Knauss, W. (1999). Creativity of Destructive Fantasies. *Group Analysis, 32 (3)*: 397–411.

Kronmüller, K. & Hartmann, M. (1997). Psychoanalytische Therapieforschung bei Kindern und Jugendlichen, in: H. Mandl (Ed.), *Bericht über den 40. Kongress der deutschen Gesellschaft für Psychologie.* Göttingen: Hogrefe.

Lanyado, M. (2004). *The Presence of the Therapist—Treating Childhood Trauma.* Hove: Brunner-Routledge.

Lanyado, M. (2006). The Playful Presence of the Therapist: Antidoting Defences in the Therapy of a Late Adopted Adolescent Girl. In: M. Lanyado and A. Horne (Eds.), *A Question of Technique.* Independent Psychoanalytic Approaches with Children and Adolescents Series. Hove, East Sussex: Routledge.

Lanyado, M. & Horne, A. (2006). *A Question of Technique—Independent Approaches with Children and Adolescents.* Hove, UK: Routledge.

Lao Tzu (translated by Stephen Mitchell, 1999). *Tao Te Ching.* London: Frances Lincoln.

Leach, E. (1986). *Social Anthropology.* Glasgow: Fontana Press.

Lewis, C.S. (2002). *Narnia Fortællingerne.* (translated from The Complete Cronicles of Narnia, 1950–1956). Copenhagen: Borgens Forlag.

Lewis, O. (1991). Paternal Absence: Psychotherapeutic Considerations in Boys. *Contemporary Psychoanalysis, 27*: 266–277.

Lheureux-Davidse, C. (2003). *L'autisme infantile ou le bruit de la rencontre.* Paris: L'Harmattan.

Lheureux-Davidse, C. (2006). Emergences du Langage Verbal chez des Enfants Autistes. *Perspectives Psychiatriques, Autismes, Nouveaux Enjeux Cliniques et Thérapeutiques, EDK, 45 (3)*: 226–230.

168   REFERENCES

Maiello, S. (1997). L'objet Sonore. Hypothèse d'une Mémoire Auditive Prénatale. *Journal de Psychanalyse de L'enfant, 20*: 40–66.

Mancia, M. (1993). The Absent Father: His Role in Sexual Deviation and in Transference. *International Journal of Psychoanalysis. 74*: 941–950.

Mann, D. (2006). Misanthropy and the Broken Mirror of Narcissism: Hatred in the Narcissistic Personality. In: C. Harding, (Ed.), *Aggression and Destructiveness—Psychoanalytic Perspectives*. London and New York: Routledge.

McDougall, J. (1989). The Dead Father. *International Journal of Psychoanalysis, 70*: 205–220.

Meltzer, D. (1967). *The Psycho-analytical Process*. Perthshire: Clunie Press, 1979.

Meltzer, D. (1975). *Explorations in Autism*. Perthshire: Rolland Harris Trust, Clunie Press.

Mitrani, J.L., (2007): Some technical implications of Klein's concept of 'premature ego development'. *The International Journal of Psychoanalysis, Vol. 88*: 825-842.

Molino, A. (1997). (Ed.) Interview with Nina Contart. In: *Freely Associated*. London: Free Association Books.

Molino, A. (1998). Slouching toward Buddhism: A Conversation with Nina Coltart. In: A. Molino (Ed.), *The Couch and the Tree. Dialogues in Psychoanalysis and Buddhism*. London: Constable and Co. Ltd.

Mook, B. (1998). Imaginative Play in Child Psychotherapy: The Relevance of Merleau-Ponty's Thought. *Journal of Phenomenological Psychology, 29 (2)*: 231–242.

Mottron, L. (2004). *L'autisme: une Autre Intelligence. Diagnostic, Cognition et Support des Personnes Autistes sans Déficience Intellectuelle*. Belgique: Pierre Mardaga éditeur.

Music, G. (2006). The Uses of a Neuroscientific Perspective. In: J. Kenrick, C. Lindsey & L. Tollemache (Eds.), *Creating New Families. Therapeutic Approaches to Fostering, Adoption, and Kinship Care*. London: Karnac Books.

Nadel, J. & Decety, J. (2002). *Imiter pour Découvrir L'humain*. Paris: PUF.

Nielsen, H.B. & Rudberg, M. (1994). *Psychological Gender and Modernity*. Scandinavian University Press.

Nitsun, M. (1996). *The Anti-Group: Destructive Forces in the Group and their Creative Potential*. London: Routledge.

Nitsun, M. (1999) Debating the Anti-Group: Commentary on Articles by Werner Knauss and Dick Blackwell. *Group Analysis 32 (3)*.

O'Connor, T., Brendenkamp, D. & Rutter, M. (1999). Attachment Disturbances and Disorders in Children Exposed to Early Severe Deprivation. *Infant Mental Health Journal, 20:* 10–29.

O'Shaughnessy, E. (1981). W.R. Bion's Theory of Thinking and new Techniques in Child Analysis. In E.B. Spillius (ed.): *Melanie Klein Today: Developments in theory and practice. Vol. 2: Mainly Practice* (pp. 177–190). London: Routledge, 1988.

Ogden, T. (1999). Analyzing Forms of Aliveness and Deadness. In: Ogden, T. *Reverie and Interpretation, Sensing Something Human,* pp. 23–63. London: Karnac Books.

Parsons, M. (2000). Vocation and Martial art. In: Akhtar, S. *The Dove that Returns, The Dove that Vanishes. Paradox and Creativity in Psychoanalysis.* London: Routledge.

Parsons, M. (2006). The Analyst's Countertransference to the Psychoanalytic Process. *International Journal of Psychoanalysis, 87 (5):* 1183–1198.

PDM Task Force (2006). *Psychodynamic Diagnostic Manual.* Silver Spring, Md.: Alliance of Psychoanalytic Organizations.

Perry, B.D., Pollard, R., Blakey, T., Baker, W. & Vigilant, D. (1995). Childhood Trauma, the Neurobiology of Adaptation and 'User-dependent' Development of the Brain: how 'States' become 'Traits'. *Infant Mental Health Journal, 16 (4):* 271–91.

Phillips, A. (1988). *Winnicott.* London: Fontana.

Pine, F. (1985). *Developmental Theory and Clinical Process.* New Haven: Yale University Press.

Poe, E.A. (1947). A Dream within a Dream. In: L. Untermeyer (Ed.), *The Albatross Book Of Living Verse. English and American Poetry from the Thirteenth Century to the Present Day.* Albatross.

Pynoos, R.S., Steinberg, A.M. & Wraith, R. (1995). A Developmental Model of Childhood Traumatic Stress. In: D. Cichetti & D.J. Cohen (Eds.), *Developmental Psychopathology, Vol. 2: Risk, Disorder, and Adaptation.* New York: Wiley.

Resnick, S. (1999). Borderline Personalities in Groups. *Group Analysis, 32 (3):* 331–347.

Ricard, M. (2007). *Happiness.* London: Atlantic Books (an imprint of Grove Atlantic).

Richards, V. (2005). *The who you Dream Yourself.* London: Karnac Books.

Rosenfeld, H. (1987). *Impasse and Interpretation. Therapeutic and Antitherapeutic Factors in the Psychoanalytic Treatment of Psychotic, Borderline, and Neurotic patients.* London and New York: Routledge.

Russ, S. (2004). *Play in Child Development and Psychotherapy. Toward Empirically Supported Practice.* London: Lawrence Erlbaum Associates.

Russel, B. (2000). *History of Western Philosophy.* London: Routledge.

Rutter, M. (1999). Psychosocial Adversity and Child Psychopathology. *British Journal of Psychiatry, 174:* 480–493.

Schore, A.N. (2003). *Affect Regulation and the Repair of the Self.* New York: Norton.

Segal, H. (1975). Notes on Symbol Formation. *International Journal of Psychoanalysis, 38:* 391–397.

Shakow, D., Hildgard, E.R., Kelly, E.L., Luchey, B., Sanford, R.N. & Shaffer, L.F. (1947). Recommended Graduate Training Program in Clinical Psychology. *American Psychologist, 2:* 539–558.

Stacey, R. (2005). Affects and Cognition in a Social Theory. *Group Analysis, 38 (1):* 159–176.

Steiner, J. (1993). *Psychic Retreats. Pathological Organizations in Psychotic, Neurotic and Borderline Patients.* London: Routledge.

Stern, D.N. (1985). *The Interpersonal World of the Infant.* New York: Basic Books.

Szapocznik, J., Murray, E., Scopetta, M., Hervis, O., Rio, A., Cohen, R., Rivas-Vazquez, A., Posada, V. & Kurtines, W. (1989). Structural Family Versus Psychodynamic Child Therapy for Problematic Hispanic Boys. *Journal of Consulting and Clinical Psychology, 57 (5):* 571–578.

Tarantelli, C.B. (2003). Life within Death: Towards a Metapsychology of Catastrophic Psychic Trauma. *International Journal Psychoanalysis, 84 (4):* 915–928.

Target, M. & Fonagy, P. (1994). The Efficacy of Psychoanalysis for Children with Emotional Disorders. *Journal American Academy Child Adolescent Psychiatry, 33:* 361–371.

Terr, L.C. (1991a). Childhood Traumas: An Outline and Overview. *American Journal Psychiatry, 148 (1):* 10–20.

Terr, L.C. (1991b). Children of Chowchilla: A study of Psychic Trauma. *Psychoanalytic Study Child, 34:* 547–623.

Trevarthen, C. (1997). Racines du Langage avant la Parole. *Devenir, 9 (3):* 73–93.

Trowell, J., Joffe, I., Campbell, J., Clemente, C., Almqvist, F., Sioninen, M., Koskenranta-Aalto, U., Weintraub, S., Kolaitis, G., Tomaras, V., Anastasopoulos, D., Grauson, K., Barnes, J. & Tsiantis, J. (2007). Childhood Depression: a Place for Psychotherapy. An Outcome Study Comparing Individual Psychodynamic Psychotherapy and Family Therapy. *European Child and Adolescent Psychiatry, 16.*

Tustin, F. (1986). *Autistic Barriers in Neurotic Patients*. London: Karnac Books.

Vandborg, M.L. (2007). Kognitiv Adfærdsterapi og Angst. *Psykolognyt*, 62: 8–13.

Weber M. (1906). *Die Protestantische Ethik und der Geist des Kapitalismus*. Bodenheim: Lichtblau K. und Weiss J, 1993.

Wilke, G. (2001). *How to be a Good Enough GP, Surviving and Thriving in the new Primary Care Organisations*. Abingdon: Radcliffe Medical Press.

Williams, M.H. (1987). *Collected Papers of Martha Harris and Esther Bick*. Perthshire: The Roland Harris Education Trust, Clunie Press.

Windaus, E. (2006). *The Position and Outcome of Research in Europe in Child and Adolescence*. Paper presented at the research workshop at the 5th EFPP conference of the Child and Adolescent Section, Berlin, Germany 10.-12. November.

Winnicott, D.W. (1947). Hate in the Countertransference. In: *Through Paediatrics to Psychoanalysis*. London: Karnac, 1984.

Winnicott, D.W. (1952). The Theory of the Parent-Infant Relationship. In: Winnicott, D.W. *The Maturational Processes and the Facilitating Environment*. London: Hogarth Press and The Institute of Psychoanalysis, 1965. (New York: International Universities Press).

Winnicott, D.W. (1958). The capacity to be alone, in: *The Maturational Processes and the Facilitating Environment*. London: Hogarth Press and The Institute of Psychoanalysis, 1965. (New York: International Universities Press).

Winnicott, D.W. (1963). Dependence in Infant Care, in Child Care, and in the Psychoanalytic Setting. In: Winnicott, D.W. *The Maturational Processes and the Facilitating Environment: Studies in the Theory of Emotional Development*. London: The Hogarth Press, 1965.

Winnicott, D.W. (1965). *The Maturational Processes and the Facilitating Environment: Studies in the Theory of Emotional Development*. London: The Hogarth Press.

Winnicott, D.W. (1969). The use of an Object and Relating through Identifications. In: *Playing and Reality* (pp. 101–111). London: Penguin Books, 1986.

Winnicott, D.W. (1971). *Playing and Reality*. London: Penguin Books, 1986 (London and New York: Routledge, 2002).

Young-Bruehl, E. (1989). *Anna Freud. A Biography*. London: Macmillan.

Zero To Three (1994). *Diagnostic Classification: 0–3. Diagnostic Classification of Mental Health and Developmental Disorders of Infancy and Early Childhood*. Washington, DC: Zero To Three.

INDEX